A Midsummer Night's Dream

JOSEPH
SOBRAN

mc Marshall Cavendish
Benchmark
New York

Cover: The Royal Shakespeare Company's 2005 production of *A Midsummer Night's Dream*

Series consultant: Richard Larkin

Marshall Cavendish
99 White Plains Road
Tarrytown, New York 10591
www.marshallcavendish.us

Library of Congress Cataloging-in-Publication Data
Sobran, Joseph.
A midsummer night's dream / by Joseph Sobran.
p. cm. — (Shakespeare explained)
Summary: "A literary analysis of the play *A Midsummer Night's Dream* by
William Shakespeare. Includes information on the history and culture of
Elizabethan England"—Provided by publisher.
Includes bibliographical references and index.
ISBN 978-0-7614-3030-8
1. Shakespeare, William, 1564-1616. Midsummer night's dream—Juvenile
literature. 2. Shakespeare, William, 1564-1616. Midsummer night's
dream—Examinations—Study guides. I. Title.
PR2827.S63 2009
822.3'3—dc22
2008007079

Photo research by: Linda Sykes
Royal Shakespeare Company:Front cover, 84: Art Parts RF: back cover, 6, 8, 13, 24, 32; Mikhall/
Shutterstock: 2-3; Neven Mendrila/Shutterstock: 3, 37; Raciro/istockphoto: 4; Michael Caven/
istockphoto: 8, 25, 38, 48, 78; Nik Wheeler/Corbis: 11; Portraitgalerie, Schloss Ambras, Innsbruck,
Austria/Erich Lessing/Art Resource, NY: 18; AA World Travel Library/Alamy: 20; Hideo Kurihara/
Alamy: 22; Corbis Sygma: 27; Andrew Fox/Corbis: 30; The Granger Collection: 37, 41; The British
Library: 43; The Everett Collection: 47; Hellestad Rune/Corbis Sygma: 54; Mario Tursi/20th
Century Fox/ The Kobal Collection: 57; Robbie Jack/Corbis: 61; John Springer Collection/Corbis:
68; Hulton Archive/istockphoto: 72; 20th Century Fox Film Corp. All rights reserved. Courtesy
Everett Collection: 77; Duncan Walker/ istockphoto: 94.

Editor: Deborah Grahame
Publisher: Michelle Bisson
Art Director: Anahid Hamparian
Series Designer: Kay Petronio

Printed in: Malaysia

135642

Contents

Shakespeare and His World

WILLIAM SHAKESPEARE, OFTEN NICKNAMED "THE BARD," IS, BEYOND ANY COMPARISON, THE MOST TOWERING NAME IN ENGLISH LITERATURE. MANY CONSIDER HIS PLAYS THE GREATEST EVER WRITTEN. HE STANDS OUT EVEN AMONG GENIUSES.

Yet the Bard is also closer to our hearts than lesser writers, and his tremendous reputation should neither intimidate us nor prevent us from enjoying the simple delights he offers in such abundance. It is as if he had written for each of us personally. As he himself put it, "One touch of nature makes the whole world kin."

Such tragedies as *Hamlet*, *Romeo and Juliet*, and *Macbeth* are world-famous, still performed on stage and in films. These and others have also been adapted for radio, television, opera, ballet, pantomime, novels, comic books, and other media. Two of the best ways to become familiar with them are to watch some of the many fine movies that have been made of them and to listen to recordings of them by some of the world's great actors.

Even Shakespeare's individual characters have a life of their own, like real historical figures. Hamlet is still regarded as the most challenging role ever written for an actor. Roughly as many whole books have been written about Hamlet, an imaginary character, as about actual historical figures such as Abraham Lincoln and Napoleon Bonaparte.

Shakespeare created an amazing variety of vivid characters. One of Shakespeare's most peculiar traits was that he loved his characters so much—even some of his villains and secondary or comic characters—that at times he let them run away with the play, stealing attention from his heroes and heroines.

So in *A Midsummer Night's Dream* audiences remember the absurd and lovable fool Bottom the Weaver better than the lovers who are the main characters. Romeo's friend Mercutio is more fiery and witty than Romeo himself; legend claims that Shakespeare said he had to kill Mercutio or Mercutio would have killed the play.

Shakespeare also wrote dozens of comedies and historical plays, as well as nondramatic poems. Although his tragedies are now regarded as his greatest works, he freely mixed them with comedy and history. And his sonnets are among the supreme love poems in the English language.

It is Shakespeare's mastery of the English language that keeps his words familiar to us today. Every literate person knows dramatic lines such as "Wherefore art thou Romeo?"; "My kingdom for a horse!"; "To be or not to be: that is the question"; "Friends, Romans, countrymen, lend me your ears"; and "What fools these mortals be!" Shakespeare's sonnets are noted for their sweetness: "Shall I compare thee to a summer's day?"

SO QUICK BRIGHT THINGS COME TO CONFUSION

SHAKESPEARE'S LANGUAGE

WITHOUT A DOUBT, SHAKESPEARE WAS THE GREATEST MASTER OF THE ENGLISH LANGUAGE WHO EVER LIVED. BUT JUST WHAT DOES THAT MEAN?

Shakespeare's vocabulary was huge, full of references to the Bible as well as Greek and Roman mythology. Yet his most brilliant phrases often combine very simple and familiar words:

"WHAT'S IN A NAME? THAT WHICH WE CALL A ROSE BY ANY OTHER NAME WOULD SMELL AS SWEET."

He has delighted countless millions of readers. And we know him only through his language. He has shaped modern English far more than any other writer.

Or, to put it in more personal terms, you probably quote his words several times every day without realizing it, even if you have never suspected that Shakespeare could be a source of pleasure to you.

So why do so many English-speaking readers find his language so difficult? It is our language, too, but it has changed so much that it is no longer quite the same language—nor a completely different one, either.

Shakespeare's English and ours overlap without being identical. He would have some difficulty understanding us, too! Many of our everyday words and phrases would baffle him.

Shakespeare, for example, would not know what we meant by a *car,* a *radio,* a *movie,* a *television,* a *computer,* or a *sitcom,* since these things did not even exist in his time. Our old-fashioned term *railroad train,* would be unimaginable to him, far in the distant future. We would have to explain to him (if we could) what *nuclear weapons, electricity,* and *democracy* are. He would also be a little puzzled by common expressions such as *high-tech, feel the heat, approval ratings, war criminal, judgmental,* and *whoopie cushion.*

So how can we call him "the greatest master of the English language"? It might seem as if he barely spoke English at all! (He would, however, recognize much of our dirty slang, even if he pronounced it slightly differently. His plays also contain many racial insults to Jews, Africans, Italians, Irish, and others. Today he would be called "insensitive.")

Many of the words of Shakespeare's time have become archaic. Words like *thou, thee, thy, thyself,* and *thine,* which were among the most common words in the language in Shakespeare's day, have all but disappeared today. We simply say *you* for both singular and plural, formal and familiar. Most other modern languages have kept their *thou.*

Sometimes the same words now have different meanings. We are apt to be misled by such simple, familiar words as *kind, wonderful, waste, just,* and *dear,* which he often uses in ways that differ from our usage.

Shakespeare also doesn't always use the words we expect to hear, the words that we ourselves would naturally use. When we might automatically say, "I beg your pardon" or just "Sorry," he might say, "I cry you mercy."

Often a glossary and footnotes will solve all three of these problems for us. But it is most important to bear in mind that Shakespeare was often hard for his first audiences to understand. Even in his own time his rich language was challenging. And this was deliberate. Shakespeare was inventing his own kind of English. It remains unique today.

A child doesn't learn to talk by using a dictionary. Children learn first by sheer immersion. We teach babies by pointing at things and saying their names. Yet the toddler always learns faster than we can teach! Even as babies we are geniuses. Dictionaries can help us later, when we already speak and read the language well (and learn more slowly).

So the best way to learn Shakespeare is not to depend on the footnotes and glossary too much, but instead to be like a baby: just get into the flow of the language. Go to performances of the plays or watch movies of them.

THE LANGUAGE HAS A MAGICAL WAY OF TEACHING ITSELF, IF WE LET IT. THERE IS NO REASON TO FEEL STUPID OR FRUSTRATED WHEN IT DOESN'T COME EASILY.

Hundreds of phrases have entered the English language from *Hamlet* alone, including "to hold, as t'were, the mirror up to nature"; "murder most foul"; "the thousand natural shocks that flesh is heir to"; "flaming youth"; "a countenance more in sorrow than in anger"; "the play's the thing"; "neither a borrower nor a lender be"; "in my mind's eye"; "something is rotten in the state of Denmark"; "alas, poor Yorick"; and "the lady doth protest too much, methinks."

From other plays we get the phrases "star-crossed lovers"; "what's in a name?"; "we have scotched the snake, not killed it"; "one fell swoop"; "it was Greek to me;" "I come to bury Caesar, not to praise him"; and "the most unkindest cut of all"—all these are among our household words. In fact, Shakespeare even gave us the expression "household words." No wonder his contemporaries marveled at his "fine filed phrase" and swooned at the "mellifluous and honey-tongued Shakespeare."

Shakespeare's words seem to combine music, magic, wisdom, and humor:

"THE COURSE OF TRUE LOVE NEVER DID RUN SMOOTH."

"HE JESTS AT SCARS THAT NEVER FELT A WOUND."

"THE FAULT, DEAR BRUTUS, IS NOT IN OUR STARS, BUT IN OURSELVES, THAT WE ARE UNDERLINGS."

"COWARDS DIE MANY TIMES BEFORE THEIR DEATHS; THE VALIANT NEVER TASTE OF DEATH BUT ONCE."

"NOT THAT I LOVED CAESAR LESS, BUT THAT I LOVED ROME MORE."

THERE ARE MORE THINGS IN HEAVEN AND EARTH, HORATIO, THAN ARE DREAMT OF IN YOUR PHILOSOPHY."

"BREVITY IS THE SOUL OF WIT."

"THERE'S A DIVINITY THAT SHAPES OUR ENDS, ROUGH-HEW THEM HOW WE WILL."

Four centuries after Shakespeare lived, to speak English is to quote him. His huge vocabulary and linguistic fertility are still astonishing. He has had a powerful effect on all of us, whether we realize it or not. We may wonder how it is even possible for a single human being to say so many memorable things.

Only the King James translation of the Bible, perhaps, has had a more profound and pervasive influence on the English language than Shakespeare. And, of course, the Bible was written by many authors over many centuries, and the King James translation, published in 1611, was the combined effort of many scholars.

EARLY LIFE

So who, exactly, was Shakespeare? Mystery surrounds his life, largely because few records were kept during his time. Some people have even doubted his identity, arguing that the real author of Shakespeare's plays must have been a man of superior formal education and wide experience. In a sense such doubts are a natural and understandable reaction to his rare, almost miraculous powers of expression, but some people feel that the doubts themselves show a lack of respect for the supremely human poet.

Most scholars agree that Shakespeare was born in the town of Stratford-upon-Avon in the county of Warwickshire, England, in April 1564. He was baptized, according to local church records, Gulielmus (William) Shakspere (the name was spelled in several different ways) on April 26 of that year. He was one of several children, most of whom died young.

His father, John Shakespeare (or Shakspere), was a glove maker and, at times, a town official. He was often in debt or being fined for unknown delinquencies, perhaps failure to attend church regularly. It is suspected that John was a "recusant" (secret and illegal) Catholic, but there is no proof.

Many scholars have found Catholic tendencies in Shakespeare's plays, but whether Shakespeare was Catholic or not we can only guess.

At the time of Shakespeare's birth, England was torn by religious controversy and persecution. The country had left the Roman Catholic Church during the reign of King Henry VIII, who had died in 1547. Two of Henry's children, Edward and Mary, ruled after his death. When his daughter Elizabeth I became queen in 1558, she upheld his claim that the monarch of England was also head of the English Church.

Did William attend the local grammar school? He was probably entitled to, given his father's prominence in Stratford, but again, we face a frustrating absence of proof, and many people of the time learned to read very well without schooling. If he went to the town school, he would also have learned the rudiments of Latin.

We know very little about the first half of William's life. In 1582, when he was eighteen, he married Anne Hathaway, eight years his senior. Their first daughter, Susanna, was born six months later. The following year they had twins, Hamnet and Judith.

At this point William disappears from the records again. By the early 1590s we find "William Shakespeare" in London, a member of the city's leading acting company, called the Lord Chamberlain's Men. Many of Shakespeare's greatest roles, we are told, were first performed by the company's star, Richard Burbage.

Curiously, the first work published under (and identified with) Shakespeare's name was not a play but a long erotic poem, *Venus and Adonis*, in 1593. It was dedicated to the young Earl of Southampton, Henry Wriothesley.

Venus and Adonis was a spectacular success, and Shakespeare was immediately hailed as a major poet. In 1594 he dedicated a longer, more serious poem to Southampton, *The Rape of Lucrece*. It was another hit, and for many years, these two poems were considered Shakespeare's greatest works, despite the popularity of his plays.

CHANTING FAINT HYMNS TO THE COLD, FRUITLESS MOON

SHAKESPEARE ON FILM: A SAMPLER

TODAY MOVIES, NOT LIVE PLAYS, ARE THE MORE POPULAR ART FORM. FORTUNATELY MOST OF SHAKESPEARE'S PLAYS HAVE BEEN FILMED, AND THE BEST OF THESE MOVIES OFFER AN EXCELLENT WAY TO MAKE THE BARD'S ACQUAINTANCE. RECENTLY, KENNETH BRANAGH HAS BECOME A RESPECTED CONVERTER OF SHAKESPEARE'S PLAYS INTO FILM.

Hamlet

Hamlet, Shakespeare's most famous play, has been well filmed several times. In 1948 Laurence Olivier won three Academy Awards—for best picture, best actor, and best director—for his version of the play. The film allowed him to show some of the magnetism that made him famous on the stage. Nobody spoke Shakespeare's lines more thrillingly.

The young Derek Jacobi played Hamlet in a 1980 BBC production of the play, with Patrick Stewart (now best known for *Star Trek, the Next Generation*) as the guilty king. Jacobi, like Olivier, has a gift for speaking the lines freshly; he never seems to be merely reciting the famous and familiar words. But whereas Olivier has animal passion, Jacobi is more intellectual. It is fascinating to compare the ways these two outstanding actors play Shakespeare's most complex character.

Franco Zeffirelli's 1990 *Hamlet*, starring Mel Gibson, is fascinating in a different way. Gibson, of course, is best known as an action hero, and he is not well suited to this supremely witty and introspective role, but Zeffirelli cuts the text drastically, and the result turns *Hamlet* into something that few people would have expected: a short, swift-moving action movie. Several of the other characters are brilliantly played.

Henry IV, Part One

The 1979 BBC Shakespeare series production does a commendable job in this straightforward approach to the play. Battle scenes are effective despite obvious restrictions in an indoor studio setting. Anthony Quayle gives jovial Falstaff a darker edge, and Tim Pigott-Smith's Hotspur is buoyed by some humor. Jon Finch plays King Henry IV with noble authority, and David Gwillim gives Hal a surprisingly successful transformation from boy prince to heir apparent.

Julius Caesar

No really good movie of *Julius Caesar* exists, but the 1953 film, with Marlon Brando as Mark Antony, will do. James Mason is a thoughtful Brutus, and John Gielgud, then ranked with Laurence Olivier among the greatest Shakespearean actors, plays the villainous Cassius. The film is rather dull, and Brando is out of place in a Roman toga, but it is still worth viewing.

Macbeth

Roman Polanski is best known as a director of thrillers and horror films, so it may seem natural that he should have done his 1971 *The Tragedy of Macbeth* as an often-gruesome slasher flick. But this is also one of the most vigorous of all Shakespeare films. Macbeth and his wife are played by Jon Finch and Francesca Annis, neither known for playing Shakespeare, but they are young and attractive in roles that are usually given to older actors, which gives the story a fresh flavor.

The Merchant of Venice

Once again the matchless Sir Laurence Olivier delivers a great performance as Shylock with his wife Joan Plowright as Portia in the 1974 TV film, adapted from the 1970 National Theater (of Britain) production. A 1980 BBC offering features Warren Mitchell as Shylock and Gemma Jones as Portia, with John Rhys-Davies as Salerio. The most recent production, starring Al Pacino as Shylock, Jeremy Irons as Antonio, and Joseph Fiennes as Bassanio, was filmed in Venice and released in 2004.

A Midsummer Night's Dream

Because of the prestige of his tragedies, we tend to forget how many comedies Shakespeare wrote—nearly twice the number of tragedies. Of these perhaps the most popular has always been the enchanting, atmospheric, and very silly masterpiece *A Midsummer Night's Dream*.

In more recent times several films have been made of *A Midsummer Night's Dream*. Among the more notable have been Max Reinhardt's 1935 black-and-white version, with Mickey Rooney (then a child star) as Puck.

Of the several film versions, the one starring Kevin Kline as Bottom and Stanley Tucci as Puck, made in 1999 with nineteenth-century costumes and directed by Michael Hoffman, ranks among the finest, and is surely one of the most sumptuous to watch.

Othello

Orson Welles did a budget European version in 1952, now available as a restored DVD. Laurence Olivier's 1965 film performance is predictably remarkable, though it has been said that he would only approach the part by honoring, even emulating, Paul Robeson's definitive interpretation that ran on Broadway in 1943. (Robeson was the first black actor to play Othello, the Moor of Venice, and he did so to critical acclaim, though sadly his performance was never filmed.) Maggie Smith plays a formidable Desdemona opposite Olivier, and her youth and energy will surprise younger audiences who know her only from the Harry Potter films. Laurence Fishburne brilliantly portrayed Othello in the 1995 film, costarring with Kenneth Branagh as a surprisingly human Iago, though Irène Jacob's Desdemona was disappointingly weak.

Romeo and Juliet

This, the world's most famous love story, has been filmed many times, twice very successfully over the last generation. Franco Zeffirelli directed a hit version in 1968 with Leonard Whiting and the rapturously pretty Olivia Hussey, set in Renaissance Italy. Baz Luhrmann made a much more contemporary version, with a loud rock score, starring Leonardo Di Caprio and Claire Danes, in 1996.

It seems safe to say that Shakespeare would have preferred Zeffirelli's movie, with its superior acting and rich, romantic, sun-drenched Italian scenery.

The Tempest

A 1960 Hallmark Hall of Fame production featured Maurice Evans as Prospero, Lee Remick as Miranda, Roddy McDowall as Ariel, and Richard Burton as Caliban. The special effects are primitive and the costumes are ludicrous, but it moves along at a fast pace. Another TV version aired in 1998 and was nominated for a Golden Globe. Peter Fonda played Gideon Prosper and Katherine Heigl played his daughter Miranda Prosper. Sci-Fi fans may already know that the classic 1956 film *Forbidden Planet* is modeled on themes and characters from the play.

Twelfth Night

Trevor Nunn adapted the play for the 1996 film he also directed in a rapturous Edwardian setting, with big names like Helena Bonham Carter, Richard E. Grant, Imogen Stubbs, and Ben Kingsley as Feste. A 2003 film set in modern Britain provides an interesting multicultural experience; it features an Anglo-Indian cast with Parminder Nagra (*Bend It Like Beckham*) playing Viola. For the truly intrepid, a twelve-minute silent film made in 1910 does a fine job of capturing the play through visual gags and over-the-top gesturing.

THESE FILMS HAVE BEEN SELECTED FOR SEVERAL QUALITIES: APPEAL AND ACCESSIBILITY TO MODERN AUDIENCES, EXCELLENCE IN ACTING, PACING, VISUAL BEAUTY, AND, OF COURSE, FIDELITY TO SHAKESPEARE. THEY ARE THE MOTION PICTURES WE JUDGE MOST LIKELY TO HELP STUDENTS UNDERSTAND THE SOURCE OF THE BARD'S LASTING POWER.

SHAKESPEARE'S THEATER

Today we sometimes speak of "live entertainment." In Shakespeare's day, of course, all entertainment was live, because recordings, films, television, and radio did not yet exist. Even printed books were a novelty.

In fact, most communication in those days was difficult. Transportation was not only difficult but slow, chiefly by horse and boat. Most people were illiterate peasants who lived on farms that they seldom left; cities grew up along waterways and were subject to frequent plagues that could wipe out much of the population within weeks.

Money—in coin form, not paper—was scarce and hardly existed outside the cities. By today's standards, even the rich were poor. Life

ELIZABETH I, A GREAT PATRON OF POETRY AND THE THEATER, WROTE SONNETS AND TRANSLATED CLASSIC WORKS.

was precarious. Most children died young, and famine or disease might kill anyone at any time. Everyone was familiar with death. Starvation was not rare or remote, as it is to most of us today. Medical care was poor and might kill as many people as it healed.

This was the grim background of Shakespeare's theater during the reign of Queen Elizabeth I, who ruled from 1558 until her death in 1603. During that period England was also torn by religious conflict, often violent, among Roman Catholics who were loyal to the Pope, adherents of the Church of England who were loyal to the queen, and the Puritans who would take over the country in the revolution of 1642.

Under these conditions, most forms of entertainment were luxuries that were out of most people's reach. The only way to hear music was to be in the actual physical presence of singers or musicians with their instruments, which were primitive by our standards.

One brutal form of entertainment, popular in London, was bear-baiting. A bear was blinded and chained to a stake, where fierce dogs called mastiffs were turned loose to tear him apart. The theaters had to compete with the bear gardens, as they were called, for spectators.

The Puritans, or radical Protestants, objected to bear-baiting and tried to ban it. Despite their modern reputation, the Puritans were anything but conservative. Conservative people, attached to old customs, hated them. They seemed to upset everything. (Many of America's first settlers, such as the Pilgrims who came over on the *Mayflower*, were dissidents who were fleeing the Church of England.)

Plays were extremely popular, but they were primitive, too. They had to be performed outdoors in the afternoon because of the lack of indoor lighting. Often the "theater" was only an enclosed courtyard. Probably the versions of Shakespeare's plays that we know today were not used in full, but shortened to about two hours for actual performance.

But eventually more regular theaters were built, featuring a raised stage extending into the audience. Poorer spectators (illiterate "groundlings") stood on the ground around it, at times exposed to rain and snow. Wealthier people sat in raised tiers above. Aside from some costumes, there were few props or special effects and almost no scenery. Much had to be imagined: Whole battles might be represented by a few actors with swords. Thunder might be simulated by rattling a sheet of tin offstage.

The plays were far from realistic and, under the conditions of the time, could hardly try to be. Above the rear of the main stage was a small balcony. (It was this balcony from which Juliet spoke to Romeo.) Ghosts and witches might appear by entering through a trapdoor in the stage floor.

Unlike the modern theater, Shakespeare's Globe Theater—he describes it as "this wooden O"—had no curtain separating the stage from the audience. This allowed intimacy between the players and the spectators.

THE RECONSTRUCTED GLOBE THEATER WAS COMPLETED IN 1997 AND IS LOCATED IN LONDON, JUST 200 YARDS (183 METERS) FROM THE SITE OF THE ORIGINAL.

THAT WOULD HANG US, EVERY MOTHER'S SON

The spectators probably reacted rowdily to the play, not listening in reverent silence. After all they had come to have fun! And few of them were scholars. Again, a play had to amuse people who could not read.

The lines of plays were written and spoken in prose or, more often, in a form of verse called iambic pentameter (ten syllables with five stresses per line). There was no attempt at modern realism. Only males were allowed on the stage, so some of the greatest women's roles ever written had to be played by boys or men. (The same is true, by the way, of the ancient Greek theater.)

Actors had to be versatile, skilled not only in acting, but also in fencing, singing, dancing, and acrobatics. Within its limitations, the theater offered a considerable variety of spectacles.

Plays were big business, not yet regarded as high art, sponsored by important and powerful people (the queen loved them as much as the groundlings did). The London acting companies also toured and performed in the provinces. When plagues struck London, the government might order the theaters to be closed to prevent the spread of disease among crowds. (They remained empty for nearly two years from 1593 to 1594.)

As the theater became more popular, the Puritans grew as hostile to it as they were to bear-baiting. Plays, like books, were censored by the government, and the Puritans fought to increase restrictions, eventually banning any mention of God and other sacred topics on the stage.

In 1642 the Puritans shut down all the theaters in London, and in 1644 they had the Globe demolished. The theaters remained closed until Charles's son King Charles II was restored to the throne in 1660 and the hated Puritans were finally vanquished.

But, by then, the tradition of Shakespeare's theater had been fatally interrupted. His plays remained popular, but they were often rewritten by inferior dramatists and it was many years before they were performed (again) as he had originally written them.

THE ROYAL SHAKESPEARE THEATER, IN STRATFORD-UPON-AVON, WAS CLOSED IN 2007. A NEWLY DESIGNED INTERIOR WITH A 1000-SEAT AUDITORIUM WILL BE COMPLETED IN 2010.

Today, of course, the plays are performed both in theaters and in films, sometimes in costumes of the period (ancient Rome for *Julius Caesar*, medieval England for *Henry V*), sometimes in modern dress (*Richard III* has recently been reset in England in the 1930s).

PLAYS

In the England of Queen Elizabeth I, plays were enjoyed by all classes of people, but they were not yet respected as a serious form of art.

Shakespeare's plays began to appear in print in individual, or "quarto," editions in 1594, but none of these bore his name until 1598. Although his tragedies are now ranked as his supreme achievements, his name was first associated with comedies and with plays about English history.

The dates of Shakespeare's plays are notoriously hard to determine. Few performances of them were documented; some were not printed until decades after they first appeared on the stage. Mainstream scholars generally place most of the comedies and histories in the 1590s, admitting that this time frame is no more than a widely accepted estimate.

The three parts of *King Henry VI*, culminating in a fourth part, *Richard III*, deal with the long and complex dynastic struggle or civil wars known as the Wars of the Roses (1455–1487), one of England's most turbulent periods. Today it is not easy to follow the plots of these plays.

It may seem strange to us that a young playwright should have written such demanding works early in his career, but they were evidently very popular with the Elizabethan public. Of the four, only *Richard III*, with its wonderfully villainous starring role, is still often performed.

Even today, one of Shakespeare's early comedies, *The Taming of the Shrew*, remains a crowd-pleaser. (It has enjoyed success in a 1999 film adaptation, *10 Things I Hate About You,* with Heath Ledger and Julia Stiles.)

THE "REAL" SHAKESPEARE

AROUND 1850 DOUBTS STARTED TO SURFACE ABOUT WHO HAD ACTUALLY WRITTEN SHAKESPEARE'S PLAYS, CHIEFLY BECAUSE MANY OTHER AUTHORS, SUCH AS MARK TWAIN, THOUGHT THE PLAYS' AUTHOR WAS TOO WELL EDUCATED AND KNOWLEDGEABLE TO HAVE BEEN THE MODESTLY SCHOOLED MAN FROM STRATFORD.

Who, then, was the real author? Many answers have been given, but the three leading candidates are Francis Bacon, Christopher Marlowe, and Edward de Vere, Earl of Oxford.

Francis Bacon (1561-1626)

Bacon was a distinguished lawyer, scientist, philosopher, and essayist. Many considered him one of the great geniuses of his time, capable of any literary achievement, though he wrote little poetry and, as far as we know, no dramas. When people began to suspect that "Shakespeare" was only a pen name, he seemed like a natural candidate. But his writing style was vastly different from the style of the plays.

Christopher Marlowe (1564–1593)

Marlowe wrote several excellent tragedies in a style much like that of the Shakespeare tragedies, though without the comic blend. But he was reportedly killed in a mysterious incident in 1593, before most of the Bard's plays existed. Could his death have been faked? Is it possible that he lived on for decades in hiding, writing under a pen name? This is what his advocates contend.

Edward de Vere, Earl of Oxford (1550–1604)

Oxford is now the most popular and plausible alternative to the lad from Stratford. He had a high reputation as a poet and playwright in his day, but his life was full of scandal. That controversial life seems to match what the poet says about himself in the sonnets, as well as many events in the plays (especially *Hamlet*). However, he died in 1604, and most scholars believe this rules him out as the author of plays that were published after that date.

THE GREAT MAJORITY OF EXPERTS REJECT THESE AND ALL OTHER ALTERNATIVE CANDIDATES, STICKING WITH THE TRADITIONAL VIEW, AFFIRMED IN THE 1623 FIRST FOLIO OF THE PLAYS, THAT THE AUTHOR WAS THE MAN FROM STRATFORD. THAT REMAINS THE SAFEST POSITION TO TAKE, UNLESS STARTLING NEW EVIDENCE TURNS UP, WHICH, AT THIS LATE DATE, SEEMS HIGHLY UNLIKELY.

The story is simple: The enterprising Petruchio resolves to marry a rich young woman, Katherina Minola, for her wealth, despite her reputation for having a bad temper. Nothing she does can discourage this dauntless suitor, and the play ends with Kate becoming a submissive wife. It is all the funnier for being unbelievable.

With *Romeo and Juliet* the Bard created his first enduring triumph. This tragedy of "star-crossed lovers" from feuding families is known around the world. Even people with only the vaguest knowledge of Shakespeare are often aware of this universally beloved story. It has inspired countless similar stories and adaptations, such as the hit musical *West Side Story*.

By the mid-1590s Shakespeare was successful and prosperous, a partner in the Lord Chamberlain's Men. He was rich enough to buy New Place, one of the largest houses in his hometown of Stratford.

Yet, at the peak of his good fortune, came the worst sorrow of his life: Hamnet, his only son, died in August 1596 at the age of eleven, leaving nobody to carry on his family name, which was to die out with his two daughters.

Our only evidence of his son's death is a single line in the parish burial register. As far as we know, this crushing loss left no mark on Shakespeare's work. As far as his creative life shows, it was as if nothing had happened. His silence about his grief may be the greatest puzzle of his mysterious life, although, as we shall see, others remain.

During this period, according to traditional dating (even if it must be somewhat hypothetical), came the torrent of Shakespeare's mightiest works. Among these was another quartet of English history plays, this one centering on the legendary King Henry IV, including *Richard II* and the two parts of *Henry IV*.

Then came a series of wonderful romantic comedies: *Much Ado About Nothing*, *As You Like It*, and *Twelfth Night*.

ACTOR JOSEPH FIENNES PORTRAYED THE BARD IN THE 1998 FILM *SHAKESPEARE IN LOVE*, DIRECTED BY JOHN MADDEN.

In 1598 the clergyman Francis Meres, as part of a larger work, hailed Shakespeare as the English Ovid, supreme in love poetry as well as drama. "The Muses would speak with Shakespeare's fine filed phrase," Meres wrote, "if they would speak English." He added praise of Shakespeare's "sugared sonnets among his private friends." It is tantalizing; Meres seems to know something of the poet's personal life, but he gives us no hard information. No wonder biographers are frustrated.

Next the Bard returned gloriously to tragedy with *Julius Caesar*. In the play Caesar has returned to Rome in great popularity after his military triumphs. Brutus and several other leading senators, suspecting that Caesar means to make himself king, plot to assassinate him. Midway through the play, after the assassination, comes one of Shakespeare's most famous scenes. Brutus speaks at Caesar's funeral. But then Caesar's friend Mark Antony delivers a powerful attack on the conspirators, inciting the mob to fury. Brutus and the others, forced to flee Rome, die in the ensuing civil war. In the end the spirit of Caesar wins after all. If Shakespeare had written nothing after *Julius Caesar*, he would still have been remembered as one of the greatest playwrights of all time. But his supreme works were still to come.

Only Shakespeare could have surpassed *Julius Caesar*, and he did so with *Hamlet* (usually dated about 1600). King Hamlet of Denmark has died, apparently bitten by a poisonous snake. Claudius, his brother, has married the dead king's widow, Gertrude, and become the new king, to the disgust and horror of Prince Hamlet. The ghost of old Hamlet appears to young Hamlet, reveals that he was actually poisoned by Claudius, and demands revenge. Hamlet accepts this as his duty, but cannot bring himself to kill his hated uncle. What follows is Shakespeare's most brilliant and controversial plot.

The story of *Hamlet* is set against the religious controversies of the Bard's time. Is the ghost in hell or purgatory? Is Hamlet Catholic or Protestant? Can revenge ever be justified? We are never really given the answers to such questions. But the play reverberates with them.

THE KING'S MEN

In 1603 Queen Elizabeth I died, and King James VI of Scotland became King James I of England. He also became the patron of Shakespeare's acting company, so the Lord Chamberlain's Men became the King's Men. From this point on, we know less of Shakespeare's life in London than in Stratford, where he kept acquiring property.

In the later years of the sixteenth century Shakespeare had been a rather elusive figure in London, delinquent in paying taxes. From 1602 to 1604 he lived, according to his own later testimony, with a French immigrant family named Mountjoy. After 1604 there is no record of any London residence for Shakespeare, nor do we have any reliable recollection of him or his whereabouts by others. As always, the documents leave much to be desired.

Nearly as great as *Hamlet* is *Othello*, and many regard *King Lear*, the heartbreaking tragedy about an old king and his three daughters, as Shakespeare's supreme tragedy. Shakespeare's shortest tragedy, *Macbeth*, tells the story of a Scottish lord and his wife who plot to murder the king of Scotland to gain the throne for themselves. *Antony and Cleopatra*, a sequel to *Julius Caesar*, depicts the aging Mark Antony in love with the enchanting queen of Egypt. *Coriolanus*, another Roman tragedy, is the poet's least popular masterpiece.

SONNETS AND THE END

The year 1609 saw the publication of Shakespeare's sonnets. Of these 154 puzzling love poems, the first 126 are addressed to a handsome young man, unnamed, but widely believed to be the Earl of Southampton; the rest concern a dark woman, also unidentified. These mysteries are still debated by scholars.

Near the end of his career Shakespeare turned to comedy again, but it was a comedy of a new and more serious kind. Magic plays a large role in these late plays. For example, in *The Tempest*, the exiled duke of Milan, Prospero, uses magic to defeat his enemies and bring about a final reconciliation.

According to the most commonly accepted view, Shakespeare, not yet fifty, retired to Stratford around 1610. He died prosperous in 1616, and left a will that divided his goods, with a famous provision leaving his wife "my second-best bed." He was buried in the chancel of the parish church, under a tombstone bearing a crude rhyme:

> GOOD FRIEND, FOR JESUS SAKE FORBEARE
> TO DIG THE DUST ENCLOSED HERE.
> BLEST BE THE MAN THAT SPARES THESE STONES,
> AND CURSED BE HE THAT MOVES MY BONES.

This epitaph is another hotly debated mystery: Did the great poet actually compose these lines himself?

SHAKESPEARE'S GRAVE IN HOLY TRINITY CHURCH, STRATFORD-UPON-AVON. HIS WIFE, ANNE HATHAWAY, IS BURIED BESIDE HIM.

THE FOLIO

In 1623 Shakespeare's colleagues of the King's Men produced a large volume of the plays (excluding the sonnets and other poems) titled *The Comedies, Histories, and Tragedies of Mr. William Shakespeare* with a woodcut portrait—the only known portrait—of the Bard. As a literary monument it is priceless, containing our only texts of half the plays; as a source of biographical information it is severely disappointing, giving not even the dates of Shakespeare's birth and death.

Ben Jonson, then England's poet laureate, supplied a long prefatory poem saluting Shakespeare as the equal of the great classical Greek tragedians Aeschylus, Sophocles, and Euripides, adding that "He was not of an age, but for all time."

Some would later denigrate Shakespeare. His reputation took more than a century to conquer Europe, where many regarded him as semi-barbarous. His works were not translated before 1740. Jonson himself, despite his personal affection, would deprecate "idolatry" of the Bard. For a time Jonson himself was considered more "correct" than Shakespeare, and possibly the superior artist.

But Jonson's generous verdict is now the whole world's. Shakespeare was not merely of his own age, "but for all time."

OUT OF THIS WOOD DO NOT DESIRE TO GO.

A GLOSSARY OF LITERARY TERMS

allegory—a story in which characters and events stand for general moral truths. Shakespeare never uses this form simply, but his plays are full of allegorical elements.

alliteration—repetition of one or more initial sounds, especially consonants, as in the saying "through thick and thin," or in Julius Caesar's statement, "veni, vidi, vici."

allusion—a reference, especially when the subject referred to is not actually named, but is unmistakably hinted at.

aside—a short speech in which a character speaks to the audience, unheard by other characters on the stage.

comedy—a story written to amuse, using devices such as witty dialogue (high comedy) or silly physical movement (low comedy). Most of Shakespeare's comedies were romantic comedies, incorporating lovers who endure separations, misunderstandings, and other obstacles but who are finally united in a happy resolution.

deus ex machine—an unexpected, artificial resolution to a play's convoluted plot. Literally, "god out of a machine."

dialogue—speech that takes place among two or more characters.

diction—choice of words for tone. A speech's diction may be dignified (as when a king formally addresses his court), comic (as when the ignorant gravediggers debate whether Ophelia deserves a religious funeral), vulgar, romantic, or whatever the dramatic occasion requires. Shakespeare was a master of diction.

Elizabethan—having to do with the reign of Queen Elizabeth I, from 1558 until her death in 1603. This is considered the most famous period in the history of England, chiefly because of Shakespeare and other noted authors (among them Sir Philip Sidney, Edmund Spenser, and Christopher Marlowe). It was also an era of military glory, especially the defeat of the huge Spanish Armada in 1588.

Globe—the Globe Theater housed Shakespeare's acting company, the Lord Chamberlain's Men (later known as the King's Men). Built in 1598, it caught fire and burned down during a performance of *Henry VIII* in 1613.

hyperbole—an excessively elaborate exaggeration used to create special emphasis or a comic effect, as in Montague's remark that his son Romeo's sighs are "adding to clouds more clouds" in *Romeo and Juliet*.

irony—a discrepancy between what a character says and what he or she truly believes, what is expected to happen and what really happens, or between what a character says and what others understand.

metaphor—a figure of speech in which one thing is identified with another, such as when Hamlet calls his father a "fair mountain." (See also *simile*.)

monologue—a speech delivered by a single character.

motif—a recurrent theme or image, such as disease in *Hamlet* or moonlight in *A Midsummer Night's Dream*.

oxymoron—a phrase that combines two contradictory terms, as in the phrase "sounds of silence" or Hamlet's remark, "I must be cruel only to be kind."

personification—imparting personality to something impersonal ("the sky wept"); giving human qualities to an idea or an inanimate object, as in the saying "love is blind."

pun—a playful treatment of words that sound alike, or are exactly the same, but have different meanings. In *Romeo and Juliet* Mercutio says, after being fatally wounded, "Ask for me tomorrow and you shall find me a grave man." "Grave" could mean either a place of burial or serious.

simile—a figure of speech in which one thing is compared to another, usually using the word *like* or *as*. (See also *metaphor*.)

soliloquy—a speech delivered by a single character, addressed to the audience. The most famous are those of Hamlet, but Shakespeare uses this device frequently to tell us his characters' inner thoughts.

symbol—a visible thing that stands for an invisible quality, as poison in *Hamlet* stands for evil and treachery.

syntax—sentence structure or grammar. Shakespeare displays amazing variety of syntax, from the sweet simplicity of his songs to the clotted fury of his great tragic heroes, who can be very difficult to understand at a first hearing. These effects are deliberate; if we are confused, it is because Shakespeare means to confuse us.

theme—the abstract subject or message of a work of art, such as revenge in *Hamlet* or overweening ambition in *Macbeth*.

tone—the style or approach of a work of art. The tone of *A Midsummer Night's Dream*, set by the lovers, Bottom's crew, and the fairies, is light and sweet. The tone of *Macbeth*, set by the witches, is dark and sinister.

tragedy—a story that traces a character's fall from power, sanity, or privilege. Shakespeare's well-known tragedies include *Hamlet, Macbeth,* and *Othello.*

tragicomedy—a story that combines elements of both tragedy and comedy, moving a heavy plot through twists and turns to a happy ending.

verisimilitude—having the appearance of being real or true.

understatement—a statement expressing less than intended, often with an ironic or comic intention; the opposite of hyperbole.

SHAKESPEARE AND
A MIDSUMMER NIGHT'S DREAM

Sir John Gilbert's ▶
illustrated title page of a
late-nineteenth century
edition of the play

A MIDSUMMER DREAM

Chapter One

Shakespeare and A Midsummer Night's Dream

CHAPTER ONE

A MIDSUMMER NIGHT'S DREAM, ONE OF SHAKESPEARE'S FIRST MASTERPIECES, HAS ALWAYS BEEN ONE OF HIS MOST POPULAR PLAYS. CERTAINLY IT IS THE SILLIEST, WITH CONFUSING PAIRS OF QUARRELING LOVERS, MISCHIEVOUS FAIRIES, IGNORANT RUSTICS, AND, OF COURSE, THAT ASS'S HEAD. IT ALSO HAS SOME OF HIS SIMPLEST AND MOST ENCHANTING POETRY.

Among his best plays, *A Midsummer Night's Dream* is Shakespeare's purest comedy, furthest from tragedy, except for a brief moment in the opening scene. Many scholars suspect that he wrote the play for an important wedding around 1595, but this, though highly plausible, cannot be proven. As the title implies the whole play has the quality of a happy dream, in which there is no evil or serious danger to anyone, and everything ends happily for all concerned. Most of the action occurs in a single night.

As a rule Shakespeare borrowed his plots from known sources, usually published before 1603. Some sources were very ancient, whether historical or mythological. *A Midsummer Night's Dream* is an exception. He seems to have invented the whole story himself. The setting and some of the chief characters are nominally ancient Greek, but the fairies and homely tradesmen smack of Shakespeare's English countryside. He seems to have a special affection for this material and for the circle of friends of the simple Bottom, his greatest buffoon and one of his most endearing creations.

The play uses more rhyme than any of his other plays, lending it a unique air of enchantment. Many scholars suspect that Titania, queen of the fairies, is a playful tribute to Queen Elizabeth I herself, who was saluted in Edmund Spenser's great poem *The Faerie Queene*.

We must bear in mind that when the play was performed in the London theater, it had to be shortened and perhaps simplified somewhat; only part of the full text could be used. It was performed outdoors in the afternoon, since there were no electric lights. The lines reminding us that the action is occurring at night, by the light of the moon and stars, are necessary.

Shakespeare's theater had almost no special effects; the language and the audience's imagination had to make up for their absence. In many ways his plays are easier to perform on film than on the stage. The lines are written to be spoken loudly, since the stage was outdoors, but in film, where the microphone picks up even the lowest sounds, the lines may be spoken in a normal tone of voice, or even whispered.

LOVE LOOKS NOT WITH THE EYES, BUT WITH THE MIND

CHANGE AND REVOLUTION IN THE THEATER

In order to understand *A Midsummer Night's Dream*, as well as Shakespeare's other plays, it is a good idea to know something of their theatrical background. During the reign of Queen Elizabeth I, from 1558 to 1603, the theater became extremely popular, not only in London but throughout England. Plays had long been performed in courtyards and by law students at the Inns of Court, a collection of buildings where they lived and studied. By the 1580s, however, regular theaters were built to accommodate large crowds of spectators. Actors such as Edward Alleyn, Richard Burbage (later a partner in Shakespeare's company, the King's Men), and the clown Will Kempe became huge stars.

Plays were also acted at the queen's court and even in large private homes. Some rich lords, such as the Earl of Oxford, employed their own companies of actors in their households to entertain guests, especially on special occasions. The comical production of "Pyramus and Thisby" at Theseus's wedding in *A Midsummer Night's Dream* may reflect this custom. Plays were performed in London, of course, at the Universities of Oxford and Cambridge, and even in towns around the country by touring companies.

By 1589 a version of *Hamlet* (most scholars doubt that it was Shakespeare's version) was being performed in one of the public theaters, along with huge successes such as *The Spanish Tragedy* (thought to be written by Thomas Kyd). But until the 1590s there were almost no records of plays' performances. In 1598 Francis Meres published a list of Shakespeare's tragedies and comedies, naming six of each, *A Midsummer Night's Dream* being one of the comedies.

THE GLOBE THEATER AS IT MAY
HAVE APPEARED AT THE HEIGHT OF
SHAKESPEARE'S POPULARITY IN THE
EARLY SEVENTEENTH CENTURY

In 1599 Shakespeare's company, the Lord Chamberlain's Men (later known as the King's Men), built its own playhouse, the Globe Theater, and many of Shakespeare's greatest plays were first performed there. (A modern replica of the Globe was recently built on the original site in London; it specializes, naturally, in Shakespeare.) Other leading acting companies included Lord Strange's Men and Lord Sussex's Men. *A Midsummer Night's Dream* may have been written for a wedding in 1595; it was first printed in 1600. It was reprinted in 1619 and again in the First Folio of the collected plays in 1623.

Elizabeth I died in 1603. In 1604 the new king, James I (who was also James VI of Scotland), became the patron of the Lord Chamberlain's Men, who were then renamed the King's Men. *A Midsummer Night's Dream* was performed at James's court under the title *A Play of Robin Goodfellow* on New Year's night in 1604.

Today King James is best remembered for another literary achievement: He sponsored the greatest English translation of the Bible, the Authorized Version. Still popularly known as the King James Version, it was published in 1611. Only Shakespeare's works have had a comparable impact on the English language.

The popularity of the theater continued to grow, and by 1610 indoor theaters began to arise. In 1613 a fire destroyed the Globe during a performance of *Henry VIII*, one of Shakespeare's last plays.

THE COURSE OF TRUE LOVE NEVER DID RUN SMOOTH

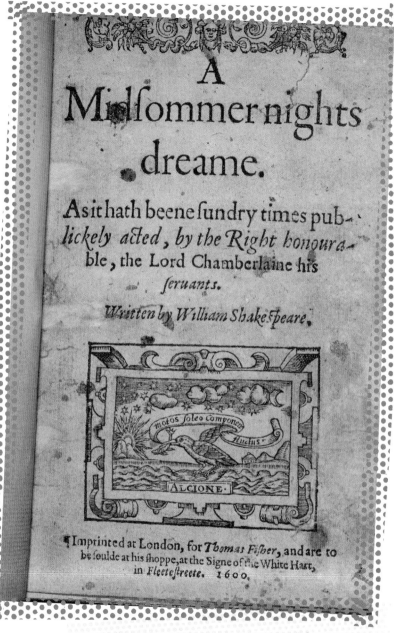

A
Midsommer nights
dreame.

As it hath beene sundry times pub-
lickely acted, by the Right honoura-
ble, the Lord Chamberlaine his
seruants.

Written by William Shakespeare.

motos soleo Componer
Huctus
ALCIONE.

¶Imprinted at London, for Thomas Fisher, and are to
be soulde at his shoppe, at the Signe of the White Hart,
in Fleetestreete. 1600.

THE TITLE PAGE OF THE PLAY, FIRST
PUBLISHED IN 1600

The drama went on flourishing until 1642, the year the Puritan Revolution overthrew King Charles I (he was beheaded in 1649) and outlawed the theaters, which the Puritans had always hated. *A Midsummer Night's Dream* kept its popularity even during the years of Puritan rule, when it was performed illegally and secretly at fairs and taverns around the English countryside.

The theaters remained closed until 1660, when the Puritans themselves were overthrown and Charles's son, Charles II, was restored to the throne. But by then Shakespeare's company was gone; the old theaters and their traditions were gone too. The theater had to start over. A new era, which was called the Restoration theater, revived Shakespeare's plays, often drastically adapting them to suit new tastes. Now plays were performed indoors at night, illuminated by candlelight. Women could legally appear upon the stage for the first time. Morals were more relaxed; the Puritans were out of power, but they remained influential.

Shakespeare's reputation declined. He was still popular, but many people, influenced by French fashions, regarded him as crude and somewhat barbarous. Samuel Pepys saw a production of *A Midsummer Night's Dream* in 1662 and wrote in his diary that it was "the most insipid ridiculous play that ever I saw in my life." Nahum Tate, England's poet

"A SWEET-FACE MAN, A PROPER MAN, AS ONE SHALL SEE IN A SUMMER'S DAY"

laureate, actually rewrote some of Shakespeare's plays completely, giving his darkest tragedy, *King Lear*, a happy ending! Tate's version was performed on the stage for more than a century, during which Shakespeare's original remained almost unknown.

Other plays by the Bard suffered the same fate. The poets John Dryden and William Davenant (who claimed to be Shakespeare's son!) were among the many people who tried to "improve" the plays but chiefly succeeded only in mutilating them. Today these supposed "improvements" are rarely performed and have been almost totally forgotten.

THE PLAY'S THE THING

- OVERVIEW AND
  ANALYSIS

- LIST OF CHARACTERS

- ANALYSIS OF MAJOR
  CHARACTERS

A lobby card of the ▶
Warner Brothers' 1935
film produced by Max
Reinhardt

Max Reinhardt's
PRODUCTION OF

A MIDSUMMER
NIGHT'S DREAM

BY WILLIAM SHAKESPEARE
MUSIC BY MENDELSSOHN

JAMES CAGNEY, JOE E. BROWN, DICK POWELL
JEAN MUIR VICTOR JORY VERREE TEASDALE
HUGH HERBERT ANITA LOUISE FRANK McHUGH
ROSS ALEXANDER IAN HUNTER MICKEY ROONEY
OLIVIA DE HAVILLAND HOBART CAVANAUGH GRANT MITCHELL

ARRANGED FOR THE SCREEN BY CHARLES KENYON & MARY C. McCALL, JR.

MAX REINHARDT AND WILLIAM DIETERLE

MUSICAL ARRANGEMENT BY
ERICH WOLFGANG KORNGOLD

DANCES DIRECTED BY NIJINSKA

COSTUMES BY MAX REE PHOTOGRAPHY BY HAL MOHR

SPECIAL PHOTOGRAPHIC EFFECTS BY FRED JACKMAN PHOTOGRAPHY BY BYRON HASKIN

66929 **Chapter
Two** 66929

CHAPTER TWO

The Play's the Thing

ACT I, SCENE 1

OVERVIEW

The story begins, appropriately, with interrupted festivity. Theseus, the duke of Athens, is about to marry Hippolyta, the queen of the Amazons (women warriors), whom he has just defeated in battle. But his loving murmurs to his bride-to-be—the wedding is only four days off—are cut short by the sudden arrival of the angry Egeus, an Athenian nobleman.

Egeus is furious because his daughter Hermia refuses to marry Demetrius, the man he has chosen for her; instead she wants to marry her lover Lysander. Egeus demands that she be put to death if she disobeys him. He petitions Theseus because as duke he represents power and is an upholder of Athenian law.

The gentle Theseus knows that the cruel law is on Egeus's side, and he warns Hermia that unless she marries Demetrius, she must either "die the death" or live the rest of her life as a nun, seeing no men, having no children, and "chanting faint hymns to the cold fruitless moon." He gives her only until his own wedding day to decide whether to marry Demetrius or to "prepare to die" for "disobedience to your father's will."

Now Lysander boldly steps forward to assert his own right to marry Hermia. Never mind the law, he tells Theseus; he loves Hermia more than Demetrius does, and she loves him, too. According to Lysander, Demetrius is also "inconstant;" he has wooed another young woman, Helena, caused her to fall madly in love with him, and then jilted her.

Theseus admits that Lysander has a point. He, too, has heard about Demetrius's dishonorable treatment of Helena, but, being busy with his own wedding plans, has had no time to inquire further. Still the law is the law. Once again he tells Hermia that she must submit to "your father's will" or choose between "death" and (softening the penalty somewhat) "a vow of single life."

"Come, my Hippolyta: what cheer, my love?" says Theseus as the case is disposed of. This line deftly suggests that Hippolyta's sympathies are with the lovers, not with the harsh law of Athens.

As the others leave to prepare for the great wedding, Hermia and Lysander remain alone together. As she weeps, he comments: "The course of true love never did run smooth." Even without external obstacles and enemies, he notes, love is often "short as any dream."

But he has a happy idea: They can run away together! He proposes that they meet in the forest outside Athens the next night. From there they can go for help to his aunt, a rich widow who lives a few miles away, beyond the reach of "the sharp Athenian law." "There, gentle Hermia," Lysander says, "may I marry thee." She joyfully agrees.

Just then Helena, Hermia's old friend and "playfellow," arrives. Helena pours out her heart, begging Hermia to tell her how she won Demetrius's love, which she wants so badly. Hermia cannot understand it herself: "I give him curses, yet he gives me love." Helena has the opposite problem: "The more I love, the more he hateth me."

Lysander and Hermia tell Helena about their plan to elope, then they leave her alone. After reflecting on the nature of love, she decides to betray her friend and reveal the elopement plan to Demetrius, hoping he will thank her as he pursues Hermia in the woods.

ANALYSIS

Egeus may seem extreme to us in demanding his daughter's death, but under ancient Greek and Roman law, a father, as head of the family (or *paterfamilias*), had the legal authority to put any member of his family to death. Usually this was done only to unwanted infants, but disobedient children and unfaithful wives might also at times be subject to this ultimate penalty. Jews and Christians were, of course, shocked by the harsh pagan law, and after the ancient world converted to Christianity, it was naturally abolished.

Writing for his Christian audience in England, Shakespeare wants us to be a little shocked, too. Will Hermia have to die? This happiest of comedies begins with that grim question. But, of course, we really know she will not die; the question is how she will escape the law. Our slight anxiety for her life is just enough to involve our sympathy and start the action of the play moving.

The four lovers are hard to tell apart. Hermia? Helena? Which is which? The close similarity of their names is a clue that Shakespeare is playing with our memories, trying to confuse us a little. Given his matchless genius for creating vivid characters, the effect here must be deliberate: four major characters are made indistinct—like figures in a dream.

Helena, when alone, speaks directly to the audience. Shakespeare often uses the soliloquy to give the audience information, to let a character express his or her innermost thoughts, or to introduce important themes of the play. On film the character may speak the soliloquy aloud (just as on the stage), or the actor may be silent, seen in close-up, while the speech is heard as a voice-over.

In this rhyming speech, Helena speaks less for herself than for the whole play:

> THINGS BASE AND VILE, HOLDING NO QUANTITY,
> LOVE CAN TRANSPOSE TO FORM AND DIGNITY.
> LOVE LOOKS NOT WITH THE EYES, BUT WITH THE MIND,
> AND THEREFORE IS WING'D CUPID PAINTED BLIND.

Just what does all this mean? It is somewhat mysterious, and for now we accept the mystery, the flow of the poetry.

Cupid was the son of Venus, goddess of love. He caused people to fall in love by shooting arrows into their hearts. Artists often represented him in pictures as either blind or blindfolded, implying that love is irrational.

Throughout the play Shakespeare reminds us of the problematic nature of love. Does it begin in the eyes or the mind? Is it above reason or below it? Wise or fickle? There is no single answer to all these questions, except that love is basic and irresistible, the joy and essence of life.

Helena speaks of "eyes" several times in this speech. This is a chief motif of the play, which contains dozens of mentions of eyes (or *eyne*, the old plural form), sight, blindness, light, darkness, day, night, sleep, waking (or "half sleep, half waking"), and, of course, dreaming—lots of dreaming. We are seldom fully sure of what is real and what is unreal.

ACT 1, SCENE 2

OVERVIEW

A group of tradesmen, ignorant yokels, gather to rehearse a play, or "interlude," to be performed at the wedding of Theseus and Hippolyta. The play is "the most lamentable comedy, and most cruel death, of Pyramus and Thisby." Actually the old story of Pyramus and Thisby is a tragedy of love, the source of Shakespeare's own *Romeo and Juliet* (which itself is often viewed as the tragic "twin" of *A Midsummer Night's Dream* for its sweet, youthful, and frequently comic flavor). Their warring families forbid them to marry, and they finally kill themselves.

The unschooled amateur actors get everything wrong. Peter Quince the carpenter is their leader, but Nick Bottom the weaver insists on stealing the show. First he wants to star as Pyramus; he promises to make the audience weep. But when Francis Flute the bellows-mender begs off on the role of "Thisby" because "I have a beard coming," Bottom offers to play that part, too. Then he decides he wants to play the roaring lion: "I will make the duke say, 'Let him roar again, let him roar again.'"

ANALYSIS

In this scene, written in homely prose befitting the low characters, Shakespeare's clowns begin to take over the play, especially the sublimely funny Nick Bottom, one of Shakespeare's greatest characters. At this point we see only Bottom's ridiculous conceit; he is funny enough, but there is no hint of the comic destiny that lies ahead for him later in the story, when the natural and the supernatural will meet and interact. Shakespeare is carefully preparing us for a delirious and unpredictable comic climax.

Just as Shakespeare loves to blend opposites, such as comedy and tragedy, here he sees to it that these bumbling actors will turn the tragedy of "Pyramus and Thisby" into a "lamentable comedy."

"MY HEART IS TRUE AS STEEL"

ACT II, SCENE 1

OVERVIEW

Oberon, king of the fairies, is estranged from his wife, Titania. They are quarreling over a little boy, a changeling "stolen from an Indian king." We learn from Puck, Oberon's chief lieutenant, that Oberon wants the boy, but that Titania refuses to give him up. After Puck has explained this to another fairy, Oberon and Titania themselves appear, he demanding the child, she still refusing. They trade accusations; she says he loves Hippolyta, and he retorts that she loves Theseus. When Titania departs Oberon summons Puck and orders him to fetch a magic flower whose juice causes sleepers to fall in love with the first live creature they see when they awaken. He will use this to take his revenge on his wife. As Puck departs Oberon makes himself invisible and watches as poor Helena pursues the scornful Demetrius, who orders her to leave. When they are gone Puck returns with the charmed flower. Oberon, pitying Helena, now directs Puck to drop its juice into the eyes of a sleeping Athenian youth. Puck promises to obey, but now the confusion begins! Oberon has neglected to tell him which person is Demetrius and which is Lysander (or which is Helena and which is Hermia).

OBERON, LEFT, PLAYED BY MICHAEL BIBERRY, AND PUCK, PLAYED BY LEE INGLEBY, PERFORMED IN 2001 AT THE ROYAL SHAKESPEARE THEATER IN LONDON.

ANALYSIS

In this scene, written in some of Shakespeare's most bewitching poetry, we enter the supernatural world of the fairies. And we find that they, like the mortals they try to dominate with their magical powers, are far from infallible. In fact they are petty, jealous, and foolish—much too sure of themselves. Greater power does not confer greater wisdom. To paraphrase Puck's most famous line: Lord, what fools these fairies be! (The wisest character in the play will turn out to be a human: Theseus.) We are touched when Demetrius cruelly insults poor, sweet Helena as she pours out her love for him. Someone is about to get his comeuppance.

ACT II, SCENE 2

OVERVIEW

Titania enters with her fairies, and she orders them to sing her to sleep. As she dozes, Oberon sneaks by and squeezes the juice of the flower onto her eyelids. As he departs, Lysander and Hermia arrive. Weary after their flight from Athens, they fall asleep—and Puck finds them. Mistaking Lysander for the Athenian youth whom Oberon had spoken of, he applies the magic flower's juice and exits, not realizing what he has done.

Now Demetrius arrives, still pursued by Helena. As he leaves her alone, she sees Lysander and wakes him. He immediately falls in love with her, tells her so, and adds that his "reason," now mature, has made him fall out of love with Hermia, for "reason says you are the worthier maid." Helena doesn't believe him; she naturally assumes that he is making cruel fun of her. She leaves, and Lysander says he is now sick of Hermia and hates her. She awakens just as he has departed, crying out to him to protect her from a serpent she has been dreaming of. But she finds he has gone.

ANALYSIS

Now this silly play—or is the whole thing just a dream?—goes into high gear. Everyone is confused; none of the characters comprehends what is going on. They have no individuality; one seems to turn into the other and back again. Shakespeare has fun keeping the audience as mixed up as the lovers. And Lysander thinks it is his "reason" that controls his heart! But worse is yet to come. We have barely met Nick Bottom.

ACT III, SCENE 1

OVERVIEW

As Titania, invisible to them, lies asleep nearby, the "actors" gather in the woods to rehearse the play that they plan to put on for the wedding of Theseus and Hippolyta. As usual Nick Bottom insists on dominating the whole production. First he objects that when Pyramus stabs himself to death, the ladies in the audience will be terrified. Therefore, he says, a prologue must be spoken to assure everyone that Pyramus is only an actor and that his suicide is not real.

Bottom raises the further objection that the lion, "a fearful wild-fowl," will also frighten the ladies. Should a second prologue be added to tell them that the beast, too, is only an actor? Again Bottom has the answer: the actor himself must be named, his face must be seen through the lion's neck, and he must address the ladies to tell them that he is not actually a lion, saying: "No, I am no such thing, I am a man as other men are."

As further problems arise, it is agreed that two other actors must impersonate the moon, by whose light Pyramus and Thisby see each other, and the wall through which they speak to each other.

Just then Puck, who is invisible on this occasion, arrives to eavesdrop.

When Bottom steps away from the group to await his cue, Puck changes Bottom's head to an ass's head without Bottom knowing it. Seeing the transformed Bottom, the other actors flee in terror, and Bottom, not understanding, thinks they are trying to scare *him*.

MICHAEL HOFFMAN'S 1999 PRODUCTION, SET IN THE NINETEENTH CENTURY, STARRED KEVIN KLINE AS BOTTOM AND MICHELLE PFEIFFER AS TITANIA.

"A LION AMONG LADIES IS A MOST DREADFUL THING"

Left alone Bottom sings. This awakens Titania, who, under the magic flower's spell, thinks she is hearing an angelic voice. Seeing Bottom she tells him that she adores his lovely voice as well as his beauty, begs him to sing again, and swears her love for him. When he replies with a joke, she coos, in all seriousness: "Thou art as wise as thou art beautiful." She summons her attendant fairies, Peaseblossom, Cobweb, Moth, and Mustardseed, to bring him fruits and honey and make him comfortable in every way. Bottom makes their acquaintance with comical courtesy, noticing nothing out of the ordinary.

ANALYSIS

This scene reaches one of Shakespeare's comic pinnacles. No reader or spectator can ever forget the play's immortal emblematic image, Bottom with an ass's head. It is as indelible as Hamlet holding poor Yorick's skull, Juliet speaking to Romeo from her balcony, or Macbeth facing the three Weird Sisters—fixed in our mind's eye forever.

The scene opens with the actors fretting absurdly about their play's going wrong if the audience fails to distinguish fiction from reality. A riot of misunderstanding ensues. When Titania professes her love to Bottom, he replies, "Methinks, mistress, you should have little reason for that. And yet, to say the truth, reason and love keep little company together nowadays." This is a shrewd comment on the whole play, and the fact that it comes incongruously from its greatest dolt is part of the fun of this comedy: Shakespeare keeps playing with the theme of love's irrationality, so, in a way, we feel that it is fitting when his most foolish character speaks the story's deepest truth.

Even Bottom's stupidity makes us like him. When the exquisite queen of the fairies falls in love with him, adoring his looks and voice, he sees nothing incongruous: To him it seems like the most natural thing in the world, and why not? He is totally unaware of his lack of beauty, intelligence, or even ordinary common sense; his misplaced self-confidence is ludicrous.

Shakespeare's low characters—those from the lower end of the social scale—are nearly always marked by crude speech, poor grammar, comic illiteracy, and verbal blunders, especially malapropisms (misused big words). Shakespeare loves to poke gentle fun at their ignorance, and they rarely get things right when it is at all possible to get them wrong.

Part of Bottom's charm is that he is completely immune to romantic love. In this respect he is the opposite of all the infatuated characters around him. He may be cruder and more stupid than they are, but he never gets carried away by his emotions. So when Titania pours out her love to him, he receives the news with perfect calm. He is polite but puzzled. Yet he has not the faintest curiosity about how this bizarre situation came to be!

ACT III, SCENE 2

OVERVIEW

Puck reports to Oberon, who is delighted to learn that the love-juice has made Titania fall in love with the absurd ass-man and, furthermore, has caused the disdainful youth to fall in love with poor Helena. But then Hermia and Demetrius enter, he begging her for love and she accusing him of murdering Lysander, which he denies. She angrily leaves him alone, and he lies down to sleep in despair.

Now Oberon and Puck realize that Puck has made a serious blunder, anointing the eyes of the wrong "Athenian youth" and causing him to fall for the wrong maiden. Oberon angrily orders Puck to go and fetch Helena at once. As soon as he is gone Oberon applies the magic juice to Demetrius's eyes.

Puck returns a moment later, followed by Lysander and Helena, who are quarreling. He is insisting that he loves her; she refuses to believe it, and accuses him of mocking her. How, she asks, can he be so fickle as to abandon Hermia? "I had no judgment when to her I swore," he replies, adding that "Demetrius loves her, and he loves not you."

Just then Demetrius wakes up, sees Helena, and makes extravagant professions of his love for her. Naturally Helena assumes that both men are cruelly making fun of her! Lysander assumes Demetrius is making fun of Helena, too, and the two men argue bitterly as Hermia arrives.

She accuses Lysander of abandoning her, and when he tells her that he now hates her and loves Helena, Helena becomes furious with her friend and concludes that all three of them have formed a "confederacy" to ridicule her. Hermia says she is amazed at this fury.

The uproar and confusion get worse until all four lovers stalk off, enraged. Oberon blames Puck for creating this unhappy situation, and orders him to produce a fog over the forest and keep the men at odds by imitating their voices until all four lovers fall asleep. Then Oberon tells Puck to use the magic juice to renew Lysander's love for Hermia. When the lovers awaken, all four will remember this whole night only as a dream.

Once everything has been straightened out, Oberon himself will go to Titania, beg her for the Indian boy, and break the spell that has made her infatuated with Bottom. All this must be accomplished before morning.

Obeying Oberon's command Puck taunts Lysander and Demetrius, separately goading them to fight until, unable to see in the fog, they lie down to sleep, exhausted. Then the two women return and fall asleep, too.

A PRODUCTION AT THE OPEN AIR THEATER IN LONDON FEATURED BOTTOM AND TITANIA SURROUNDED BY UNUSUALLY DAPPER FAIRIES SPORTING SUNGLASSES.

ANALYSIS

It is in this scene that Puck makes his famous comment: "Lord, what fools these mortals be!" The lovers' behavior, especially that of the two young men, makes this statement hard to argue with. Under the influence of the magic juice, the lovers become spectacularly "inconstant"—that is, fickle and changeable. They vow eternal love one moment, but love turns into furious hate the next. And the best part of the joke is that they attribute their sudden and arbitrary changes of mood and mind to "reason" and "judgment." They see nothing ironic in their irrational passions.

But, of course, the same is true of Titania. All of this makes the stolid Bottom seem, by comparison, a model of emotional stability. And Bottom, in his way, agrees with Puck when he observes that "reason and love keep little company together nowadays." In the midsummer night's chaos of the woods, we nearly forget the pattern of mature love represented by Theseus and Hippolyta, where love and reason do indeed seem to keep company together.

We may recall Lysander's complaint in the first scene, another of the play's most familiar lines: "The course of true love never did run smooth." When he spoke these words, however, he was thinking of tragic external obstacles and enemies (such as those faced by Romeo and Juliet or Pyramus and Thisby), not the comically insane whims of the lovers' own hearts that this story will expose.

ACT IV, SCENE 1

OVERVIEW

As the four lovers slumber, Titania tenderly caresses Bottom and orders her fairies to bring him whatever he desires. With fine formal courtesy he requests honey, hay, oats, and "a peck of provender"—a basket of feed. As for music he reveals his crude rustic taste by calling for simple musical instruments: "I have a reasonable good ear in music. Let's have the tongs and the bones." As Bottom and Titania doze off, Oberon, pitying his wife, decrees that the joke has gone far enough. Titania has also given him the Indian boy they were disputing. He tells Puck to restore Bottom's human head, while he himself breaks the spell on his queen.

Titania comes to, exclaiming that she has had a bad dream: "Methought I was enamor'd of an ass!" With a smile Oberon points to Bottom, who still has the ass's head: "There lies your love." It is time, he adds, for everyone to prepare for the great wedding in Athens. Puck restores Bottom's human head; Oberon calls for music, and all the fairies dance.

Hunting horns are heard, and Theseus arrives with Hippolyta, Egeus, and his court. Theseus and Hippolyta discuss the music made by their hounds' voices during a hunt. They discover the sleeping lovers, who then awaken. Lysander confesses that he and Hermia have come to the woods to escape the law of Athens, but before he can finish his statement, Egeus angrily interrupts him and demands that the law be brought against him in all its rigor.

Here Demetrius interrupts to tell Theseus how he came into the woods in pursuit of Hermia, but strangely found himself ceasing to love her and passionately loving Helena instead. Hearing this Theseus overrules Egeus and decrees that all the lovers—Demetrius and Helena, Lysander and Hermia—shall be married with himself and Hippolyta in Athens. As the lovers are left together, they express bafflement at what has happened, and Demetrius speaks for all of them when he says:

> "ARE YOU SURE
> THAT WE ARE AWAKE? IT SEEMS TO ME
> THAT YET WE SLEEP, WE DREAM."

Deciding that they are indeed awake, the four lovers follow Theseus and the others back to Athens, leaving the sleeping Bottom alone.

Yawning and opening his eyes, Bottom at first thinks he is rehearsing the play. Then he realizes he is alone and remembers his "vision," which he calls a "dream." He is overwhelmed by its profundity. Garbling a passage from the Bible, he says: "The eye of man hath not heard, the ear of man hath not seen, man's hand is not able to taste, his tongue to conceive, nor his heart to report what my dream was." Bottom decides that Peter Quince must write a ballad about this wondrous dream, which Bottom will sing at the end of the play.

ANALYSIS

In this scene all but one of the strands of the plots are tied up. The lovers are properly matched at last, the humane Theseus has overruled the tyrannical Egeus, Titania and Bottom are released from their spells, and everything is finally ready for the great wedding celebration we have been expecting since the play's very first lines.

Once again we see Bottom taking the most extraordinary events in stride and assuming command of Titania's fairies. His earthiness is hilariously incongruous with the enchanted atmosphere that surrounds him. We also hear of the strange harmony—the "musical discord" and "sweet thunder"—of Hippolyta's hounds' baying voices, which has been called a brilliant parallel to the blending of so many odd elements in *A Midsummer*

Night's Dream itself: the legendary Greeks, the exquisite fairies, the country bumpkins.

Topping all this is Bottom's recollection of his "dream," or "vision." He thinks it was a revelation, and he describes it in a botched version of St. Paul's promise of heaven in the first epistle to the Corinthians (2:9): "Eye hath not seen, nor ear heard, neither have entered into the heart of man, the things which God hath prepared for them that love him."

ACT IV, SCENE 2

OVERVIEW

The actors are in a tizzy. Bottom is missing! How can the play go on without the star?

Just then, Bottom shows up. Panic turns to great relief and joy. He instantly takes command of the situation. The play must proceed. He directs the actor who is playing the lion not to trim his nails, "for they shall hang out for the lion's claws." He says that the whole cast must "eat no onions nor garlic, for we are to utter sweet breath."

ANALYSIS

This is the play's shortest scene, and its serves to prepare us for the grand climax of the final act. Once again we see Bottom asserting his authority with his usual comic aplomb. Neither he nor his friends question his right to command. We have every reason to expect "Pyramus and Thisby" to be a disaster.

The scene illustrates a great comic principle: that a clever man dominating a dunce is never as funny as a dunce dominating another dunce—or a dunce dominating a clever man. Bottom's leadership of his foolish band, with unchallenged mastery, is one of Shakespeare's most inspired comic touches.

Bottom and his friends are so naïve, so free of any touch of malice, that they win our hearts; the more preposterous they are, the more we sympathize with them.

ACT V, SCENE 1

OVERVIEW

The great moment has arrived. The wedding festivities are in full swing. Theseus must choose an entertainment to fill the three hours between supper and bedtime.

Before he does so, however, he and Hippolyta discuss the strange story that the lovers have told them of the events in the woods. Theseus makes the following observation:

LOVERS AND MADMEN HAVE SUCH SEETHING BRAINS,

SUCH SHAPING FANTASIES, THAT APPREHEND

MORE THAN COOL REASON EVER COMPREHENDS.

THE LUNATIC, THE LOVER, AND THE POET

ARE OF IMAGINATION ALL COMPACT.

ONE SEES MORE DEVILS THAN VAST HELL CAN HOLD:

THAT IS THE MADMAN. THE LOVER, ALL AS FRANTIC,

SEES HELEN'S BEAUTY IN A BROW OF EGYPT.

THE POET'S EYE, IN FINE FRENZY ROLLING,

DOTH GLANCE FROM HEAVEN TO EARTH,
FROM EARTH TO HEAVEN;

AND AS IMAGINATION BODIES FORTH

THE FORMS OF THINGS UNKNOWN, THE POET'S PEN

TURNS THEM TO SHAPES, AND GIVES TO AIRY NOTHING

A LOCAL HABITATION AND A NAME.

Philostrate, master of the revels, presents a list of four plays to choose from for the evening's amusement. Theseus rejects the first three, but is attracted by the title of the fourth: "A tedious brief scene of young Pyramus and his love Thisby; very tragical mirth."

Philostrate tries to dissuade Theseus from choosing that one; he has seen it rehearsed, and the poor workmen who acted it (Bottom and company) were so bad, he says, that he laughed until he cried.

That does it. Theseus insists on "Pyramus and Thisby." Philostrate protests that it would be cruel to make fun of the poor men; Hippolyta agrees with him. But Theseus replies that the true kindness to these men will be to accept their well-meaning offer. Their intentions matter more than their actual performance. Theseus is gracious enough to be pleased by their mere desire to please. As he explains to Hippolyta,

OUR SPORT SHALL BE TO TAKE WHAT THEY MISTAKE;
AND WHAT POOR DUTY CANNOT DO, NOBLE RESPECT
TAKES IT IN MIGHT, NOT MERIT.
WHERE I HAVE COME, GREAT CLERKS HAVE PURPOSED
TO GREET ME WITH PREMEDITATED WELCOMES;
WHERE I HAVE SEEN THEM SHIVER AND LOOK PALE,
MAKE PERIODS IN THE MIDST OF SENTENCES,
THROTTLE THEIR PRACTICED ACCENT IN THEIR FEARS,
AND, IN CONCLUSION, DUMBLY HAVE BROKE OFF,
NOT PAYING ME A WELCOME. TRUST ME, SWEET,
OUT OF THIS SILENCE YET I PICK'D A WELCOME,
AND IN THE MODESTY OF FEARFUL DUTY
I READ AS MUCH AS FROM THE RATTLING TONGUE
OF SAUCY AND AUDACIOUS ELOQUENCE.
LOVE, THEREFORE, AND TONGUE-TIED SIMPLICITY
IN LEAST SPEAK MOST, TO MY CAPACITY.

MAX REINHARDT'S 1935 FILM SHOWCASED A WHO'S-
WHO OF THAT YEAR'S HOLLYWOOD ROYALTY,
INCLUDING JAMES CAGNEY, ARTHUR TREACHER,
JOE E. BROWN, DICK POWELL, AND MICKEY ROONEY.

We have to read this speech carefully several times to grasp its simple point: Theseus is saying that on occasions when great scholars ("clerks") have tried to greet him with well-rehearsed speeches, they were so nervous that they forgot their lines, but he appreciated their sincerity and overlooked their failure. In the same spirit he will pardon the bumbling actors who are trying, however ineptly, to please the wedding party tonight.

And it is a good thing he takes this tolerant attitude, for the actors quickly prove that they need plenty of tolerance! Peter Quince delivers the play's prologue, misreading his lines (because he cannot even handle the punctuation properly) so that he actually reverses their meaning.

It gets worse. The actors playing Pyramus, Thisby, the lion, the moonshine, and the wall are so bad that the audience dissolves into laughter. Hippolyta calls the play "the silliest stuff that ever I heard."

Theseus wisely replies, "The best in this kind are but shadows, and the worst are no worse if imagination amend them." That is, even the best actors are only pretending, so if we use our imaginations, we can enjoy the worst just as well. Why complain? Enjoy the illusion!

And enjoy it the audience does, joking uproariously at the talking lion, the talking wall, and the talking moonshine. The play is a great success in spite of itself. After Pyramus and Thisby have stabbed themselves and died, the lion offers to deliver an epilogue, but Theseus assures him that this will be unnecessary. It is midnight, time for bed. After a brief dance everyone retires for the night.

Puck enters to address the real audience, us. He delivers an eerily beautiful little rhyme about creatures of the night—the lion, wolf, screech owl, and ghosts released from their graves. Oberon, Titania, and the other fairies appear and all of them sing and dance until Oberon pronounces a solemn blessing on the married couples and the children they will have. Then everyone but Puck departs.

Puck apologizes for the play, asking our pardon "if we shadows have offended" and promising to make amends. After all it has been only a "dream." He begs our applause and bids us good night.

"FRESH DAYS OF LOVE ACCOMPANY YOUR HEARTS!"

CUPID IS A KNAVISH LAD, THUS TO MAKE POOR FEMALES MAD

ANALYSIS

Act V is the grand finale of Shakespeare's sweetest comedy, his least dramatic drama, his most joyous, and, some have even said, his greatest work of all. It brings together nearly all the main characters; only Egeus, the tyrannical father who threatened the lovers' happiness, is missing. The wise and humane Theseus is fully in command of the human world.

Theseus opens the act with his famous speech disparaging imagination as the faculty that marks "the lunatic, the lover, and the poet." Yet, moments later, to excuse the poor actors, he notes that they are no worse than the best actors "if imagination"—that is, the audience's imagination—"amend them." He judges them with mercy. Reason, justice, love, and imagination, at odds throughout the play, are finally harmonized.

Shakespeare's supreme tragedies are justly renowned for their profound studies of human character and fate. *A Midsummer Night's Dream* displays his genius in an amazingly different way.

If we go to this play expecting the excellences of those tragedies, we will only be disappointed and baffled. The story hardly matters; the characters seem trivial, almost interchangeable; what predominates is the mood of total enchantment in which anything can happen. The key terms and symbols are *love*, *strange*, *mad*, *moon*, and, of course, *dream*.

The tragedy *A Midsummer Night's Dream* most resembles and sometimes reminds us of is *Romeo and Juliet*, and Lysander puts us in mind of that tragedy in the opening scene when he offers the moral that "the course of true love never did run smooth." But this world-famous observation turns out to be a joke, foreshadowing the very opposite of tragedy. Lysander, whose heart veers suddenly from Hermia to Helena and back to Hermia again, stands for anything but "true love." His love is fickleness itself, the plaything of Puck and the magic flower. There is a terrible logic of doom in a play like *Macbeth*, where every step the hero takes leads to his damnation, but in this play, all the events are light and arbitrary, and damnation seems impossible. In *Macbeth*, the hero is the villain; in this comedy, there are no villains, and villainy itself can hardly exist. The worst mischief is Puck's playful meddling.

It is because there is so little real suspense in *A Midsummer Night's Dream* that it has the permanent, even eternal, quality of myth: we remember its supernatural atmosphere, and especially the incident involving Bottom and Titania, long after we have lost any curiosity about how the very slight story will turn out.

IT IS NOT ENOUGH TO SPEAK, BUT TO SPEAK TRUE

LIST OF CHARACTERS

Noble Characters

Theseus, duke of Athens

Hippolyta, queen of the Amazons and bride of Theseus

Egeus, an Athenian nobleman, father of Hermia

Lysander, lover of Hermia

Demetrius, suitor of Hermia, approved by Egeus

Philostrate, Theseus's master of the revels

Hermia, daughter of Egeus, in love with Lysander

Helena, in love with Demetrius

Fairies

Oberon, king of the fairies

Titania, queen of the fairies

Puck (Robin Goodfellow)

Peaseblossom, Cobweb, Moth, Mustardseed (minor fairies)

Tradesmen (actors)

Peter Quince, a carpenter

Nick Bottom, a weaver

Francis Flute, a bellows-mender

Tom Snout, a tinker

Snug, a joiner

Robin Starveling, a tailor

ANALYSIS OF MAJOR CHARACTERS

For reasons we will consider later, the characters of *A Midsummer Night's Dream*, unlike those of Shakespeare's tragedies, offer us little to analyze. Whole books have been written about Hamlet alone; but nobody would write a book about Puck or Bottom the Weaver!

THESEUS

Theseus seems, at first glance, to be the most important character in the play, the wise and reasonable ruler of Athens. The others appeal to him to settle their disputes; at his climactic wedding, he graciously accepts the tradesmen's bungling attempt to please him with their preposterous play.

HIPPOLYTA

Hippolyta, Theseus's bride, is queen of the Amazons, legendary warrior women, but she shows none of her ferocity here; rather, she is a highly civilized and sympathetic figure who speaks very few words and has little effect on the play's action.

THE FOUR LOVERS

Lysander, Demetris, Hermia, and Helena have so little individuality that we can barely tell them apart. And this is surely deliberate on Shakespeare's part, since he is unsurpassed at creating characters of the greatest depth and complexity when he wants to. In this play he is doing something utterly different from what he does in his tragedies, where the plots are driven by human choice, and character is fate. Here fate is magical and whimsical, and the fairies are in control. Rounded, three-dimensional figures would be out of place and would destroy the spell of the poetry.

OBERON AND TITANIA

Oberon and Titania, king and queen of the fairies, are nearly as silly as the human lovers. Puck, Oberon's mischievous lieutenant, exists only to perform pranks and cast charms on the humans, while speaking some of Shakespeare's simplest and most exquisite verse—of bats, owls, spiders, crabs, geese, worms, larks, mice, serpents, cowslips, acorns, and other homely natural things. More than any other character, he creates the play's atmosphere of night and enchantment.

BOTTOM THE WEAVER

Bottom the Weaver steals the show, though not in the way he intends to. He has absolutely no sense of the magical and supernatural forces around him. Stolid and practical he remains completely unaware of his own transformation into an ass. When Puck restores his human head and releases Titania from the spell of the flower's juice, Bottom thinks he has had an amazing "vision" in a dream. He is totally immune to love; he believes he is a great actor who will move the courtly audience to deep emotion. His stupidity is obvious to everyone but him and his equally obtuse friends, who admire him greatly. In a sense Bottom's invincible self-image is the biggest joke of the play! When the story, the poetry, and the other characters bewitch us, he brings us back to earthy reality.

And yet Shakespeare lets this clown have the most profound insight into love and imagination, when he awakens to speak of his "most rare vision." Among all Shakespeare's comic characters, only Falstaff rivals Bottom. It is hard to say which of the two is the greater comic giant.

A CLOSER LOOK

- THEMES

- MOTIFS

- SYMBOLS

- LANGUAGE

- INTERPRETING THE PLAY

A lobby card of 20th ▶
Century Fox's 1999
production includes
the teaser line, "Love
makes fools of us all."

RUPERT
EVERETT

CALISTA
FLOCKHART

KEVIN
KLINE

MICHELLE
PFEIFFER

STANLEY
TUCCI

A WILLIAM
SHAKESPEARE'S
MIDSUMMER
NIGHT'S

66929 **Chapter Three** 66929

CHAPTER THREE

A Closer Look

THEMES

The chief theme of *A Midsummer Night's Dream*, to put it very prosaically, is that love is irrational. Poets and lovers may talk about true love, but in this play, love is utterly whimsical, at the mercy of fairies and flowers. The lovers may delude themselves into thinking that their love is the product of reason and can never change; we know better. We see Lysander pledge his eternal devotion to Hermia, and then, awaking after Puck has anointed his eyes, abruptly switch his affections to Helena, with this comical explanation:

> NOT HERMIA, BUT HELENA I LOVE.
> WHO WILL NOT CHANGE A RAVEN FOR A DOVE?
> THE WILL OF MAN IS BY HIS REASON SWAY'D,
> AND REASON SAYS YOU ARE THE WORTHIER MAID.

Obviously reason has nothing to do with it. No wonder Helena thinks Lysander is making a cruel joke of her. Her suspicion is doubled when Demetrius, who has threatened to kill or violate her, also pours out his love: "O Helen, goddess, nymph, perfect, divine!" Then she thinks Hermia has also joined the two men in a conspiracy (or "confederacy") to mock her.

MOTIFS

A Midsummer Night's Dream is marked by dizzying repetition of interrelated key words, many of them contrasting (or ambiguously related to each other): dreaming and waking, sleep and death, eyes and blindness, moon and light, night and day, magic and music, songs and shrieks, tears and laughter, wisdom and folly, judgment and imagination, Venus and Cupid, comedy and tragedy, sport and illusion, love and hate, love and law, love and reason. Used countless times, they set a definite tone, but they also keep us confused and off balance. The elements are simple, yet too abundant for us to grasp fully—"more than cool reason ever comprehends," like dreams within a dream. Our minds are overwhelmed—as Shakespeare means them to be. He never intended his audience to take it all in. Our confusion is the very effect he intended when he wrote the play; we should never feel stupid for being confused.

In all Shakespeare's plays—we can never repeat this too often—Shakespeare's language is deliberately too dense for easy understanding. We only glimpse his full meaning. Each rereading yields us fuller glimpses of a play's real depth. No simple paraphrase or translation can possibly give us all of it. Is it confusing? Of course. It is supposed to be. Shakespeare makes us laugh at our own confusion.

Like many of Shakespeare's comedies, this one moves from the "normal" world (Athens, in this case—the realm of law, order, and reason), to an enchanted one (the nocturnal forest ruled by the fairies), then back to the normal one (where magic becomes the marriage festivity). Which one is the real world? Even this is left in doubt at the end, when Puck tells us that the whole story has been a dream!

We may compare *As You Like It*, which begins in the normal court world, moves to the enchanted Forest of Arden (where the love story occurs and the characters are transformed, though without magic), and back to the world of the court; and *The Tempest*, where the whole story takes place on an enchanted island—though we learn that the action really began back in Milan, Italy, the "normal" world, where, at the story's end, the transformed characters will return to normal life, leaving magic behind. (There is even a figure like Puck, the sexless spirit Ariel, who obeys the magician-hero Prospero, in whom Shakespeare seems to combine Oberon and Theseus.)

Other Shakespearean comedies follow the same pattern, whether supernatural action is overt, merely implied, or faintly suggested by the outline of the story. Some are as realistic as *The Two Gentlemen of Verona*, some as otherworldly as *The Winter's Tale*. Shakespeare's comedies, with all their rich variations, display the astounding versatility of his genius. How could a single imagination create so much? "After God," one critic has marveled, "Shakespeare has created most." Yet he never simply repeats a successful formula; each of his masterpieces is something totally, miraculously new.

Shakespeare's tragedies observe a similar pattern, from normal to abnormal and back again. In *Hamlet*, for example, a mysterious ghost in armor, looking like the late King Hamlet and accompanied by feverish preparations for war, interrupts the peaceful life of Denmark; then we see the royal court of the new king, unaware of this strange eruption. The ghost tells Prince Hamlet a terrible secret, and the real story begins. After much violence and intrigue, Denmark seems to return to normal, only to explode in a final scene of violence and death. Then Norway conquers Denmark, and the tragedy ends in real peace.

Even *King Lear*, the darkest of Shakespeare's tragedies, follows something like this comic outline. The action begins at Lear's apparently normal court, where he tries, foolishly, to divide his kingdom peacefully among his three daughters, two of whom despise him. When this scheme results in chaos, with the banishment of his only true-hearted daughter, Cordelia, and the faithful earl of Kent, he is forced to flee to the wilderness with his fool, where he goes mad and is transformed by suffering into a wiser man. After his terrible ordeal, which ends in death, the play returns to a desolate normality, in which it ends.

And in *Lear* too, Shakespeare's language, for the most part, is deliberately complex; it is simplest only in the most crucial and emotional scenes. The tremendous, heart-rending scene in which Lear and Cordelia are reunited is written in some of the plainest words he ever wrote: "You do me wrong to take me out of the grave. . . . I know you do not love me . . ." The same is true when Othello says, "My heart is turned to stone. I strike it, and it hurts my hand. . . . But yet the pity of it, Iago! O Iago, the pity of it, Iago!" (One reason for Shakespeare's many songs, especially in the comedies, is to clarify and intensify his emotional meaning as much as possible.) And, of course, Hamlet speaks the simplest and most famous sentence in the English language: "To be or not to be: that is the question."

SYMBOLS

In *A Midsummer Night's Dream*, the characters themselves are hardly more than symbols. Theseus represents human rationality and the ideal of civility; the four nearly identical lovers stand for the folly and fickleness of love; Puck stands for the playful whimsy of Fairyland; and Bottom stands for innocent and lovable stupidity. Venus, of course, is the goddess of love; her son Cupid symbolizes love's arbitrary randomness. Phoebe, goddess of the moon, governs the earth's waters, which also represent both purification and change.

LANGUAGE

If Shakespeare seems hard for us to read without plenty of footnotes, we should always bear in mind that he would need far more footnotes to read modern English than we need to read him. He would find us baffling. We must beware of the assumption that his language merely reflects the way English people spoke spontaneously "in those days." It does not. (We will say more on this later.)

Shakespeare's language sounds "artificial" to our modern ears, and that is for a very good reason: It *is* artificial. It is deliberately artificial.

And right at the beginning, if we want to understand Shakespeare at all, we must get rid of a very silly modern prejudice: the notion that art should always be "natural" and that whatever is artificial is phony. The very words *art* and *artificial* (along with *artifice* and others) are obviously related.

In *The Adventures of Huckleberry Finn*, a comic masterpiece in its own right, though vastly different from *A Midsummer Night's Dream*, Mark Twain has immense fun with the way Shakespeare sounded to illiterate people on the American frontier. The fraudulent "duke" whom Huck and Jim encounter on the Mississippi River plans to make a fortune by presenting bogus productions of Shakespeare to the local rubes, featuring a mangled version of Hamlet's soliloquy. He patches together famous lines from the tragedies, not realizing that he has completely misunderstood them. (Huck doesn't understand them, either; he takes everything quite seriously.) The "duke" is nearly as ignorant as his intended victims.

Shakespeare's formal English is a foreign language to Twain's yokels. Twain's ultimate joke, a sophisticated one, is that these yokels are overawed by genuinely literary language; they understand only crudely plain and practical English, and they mistake anything else for refined eloquence, no matter how absurd it may be. All the characters in *Huckleberry Finn*, you might say, exist on the same intellectual level as Bottom the Weaver. They are completely unprepared for real art, which is artificial.

It is impossible, by definition, for art *not* to be artificial. Even the crudest lyrics of rap music are artificial. After all they rhyme. They may seem "natural" when compared with the lyrics of the old songs of

I'LL PUT A GIRDLE ROUND ABOUT THE EARTH IN FORTY MINUTES

THE ROYAL SHAKESPEARE COMPANY'S MOODY, IMAGINATIVE TAKE ON THE PLAY INCORPORATES NAKED DOLLS AS FAIRIES, MANIPULATED BY BLACK-CLAD ACTORS.

Broadway musicals, but this is only relative. Rhyme and fixed rhythms are a highly unnatural form of expression, so even the difference between rap and grand opera is, in the end, merely a matter of degree. The so-called realism we usually prefer is just a matter of taste; we expect art to stress its realism and to conceal, as much as possible, its artifice.

Consider a classic movie like *The Godfather*. When it was released in 1972, it seemed like the ultimate in realism, with its violence, its frank sexuality, its raw language, its breaking of old taboos, and various other shocking departures from the conventions of older gangster films. Suddenly everything before it seemed quaint; at the time, it was the most exciting film ever made—but only for a while. It was followed by far more graphic gangster films (such as *Goodfellas*, for example) that now make it, in turn, seem rather quaint and artificial to today's audiences. The original shock is gone.

This may be a good place to emphasize our earlier point. If Shakespeare could see *The Godfather*, he would need a huge book, many times longer than this one, to make it comprehensible to him. He knew nothing of a thousand details that we take for granted: inventions such as the automobile and the electric light, historical events such as World War II (or even the existence of New York City, with all its immigrant groups), not to mention all the technology of motion pictures (with everything from photography to sound recording); the list, after four centuries, is endless.

There has been a certain analogy in Shakespearean acting styles. Until the 1930s the dominant style was the lyrical and intellectual one typified by John Gielgud. Then Laurence Olivier popularized an earthier, more explosive, even animalistic style that overnight made Gielgud's seem old-fashioned; for a full generation Olivier was widely considered the greatest actor in the world, his career culminating in 1965 with his magnificently fiery Othello. But today even Olivier's style—what his friend Ralph Richardson called "Larry's splendid fury"—has begun to appear out of date. Eventually every generation's latest fashion becomes old hat.

The English language, of course, has changed almost beyond recognition since 1600. And the world has become enormously more complex. But Shakespeare's own vocabulary and style were never easy for audiences to grasp. He never meant them to be.

This is where Shakespeare's artificiality becomes so important. He wrote in a consciously heightened style that was unlike everyday speech. Most of his characters speak in blank verse—lines of ten syllables, usually unrhymed—while some speak in rhyme. Others, especially low characters like Bottom and his friends, speak in prose, which may be comically illiterate, but even this is artificial and far from the way people actually talked in normal conversation.

In *A Midsummer Night's Dream*, Shakespeare created imaginary styles of expression that were suitable to the imaginary world and the fantastic characters he was creating. Theseus, Puck, and Bottom are all equally "unnatural" in their different ways, just as the fantastic characters in Mozart's great opera *The Magic Flute* all sing in styles that are appropriate both to themselves and to the work as a whole. Like Shakespeare's comedy, Mozart's opera is about enchantment (its French title is *La Flûte Enchantée*).

I HAVE HAD A DREAM, PAST THE WIT OF MAN TO SAY WHAT DREAM IT WAS.

"THE WISEST AUNT, TELLING THE SADDEST TALE"

Movies, stemming from photography, almost demand realism. Other art forms, however, such as ballet, have their roots in ritual and virtually require a more formal approach. Attempts to make opera naturalistic, for example, have usually failed. If your taste in the performing arts runs to gritty film noir, you are unlikely to care for slapstick comedy. Such forms are equally stylized, but they cannot be combined.

Finally we may ask why tragedy is supposed to be more real—and realistic—than comedy. Are tears more true to life than laughter? Is the morbid preferable to the ordinary, the nonexistent more fundamental than the actual? Is grief more basic than joy? And is death more "real" than life?

Obviously the answer to all these questions is no. It can never be yes. So why has the dark and tragic in art—the "realistic"—become more prestigious than the bright, the joyful, the comic?

One possible practical reason is that tragedy focuses on the individual, while comedy is concerned with the entire society, so that the tragic actor (Olivier, for example) receives more attention, fame, and glory than any group or ensemble of performers.

At any rate Shakespeare shows the most total command of both modes, tragic and comic. Neither is necessarily more "natural" than the other. Shakespeare blended them brilliantly, and his contemporaries praised him as an excellent "imitator of nature."

INTERPRETING THE PLAY

SHAKESPEAREAN COMEDY

A Midsummer Night's Dream is, in a sense, Shakespeare's purest comedy. According to an old and stubborn idea, Shakespeare wrote comedies when he was in a happy mood and tragedies when he was in a more somber frame of mind, entering a "tragic period" during a time of personal troubles. One critic rightly ridiculed this notion under the heading of "the mythical sorrows of Shakespeare."

Today most scholars agree that Shakespeare was an artist whose works may not correspond at all to his personal feelings when he wrote them. An architect may design a mansion or a cathedral, but which he chooses to do probably has nothing to do with whether he is in a religious mood when he decides. It may be simply a matter of which he has been asked or hired to do.

A Midsummer Night's Dream, for all we know, may have been written for an important wedding celebration. We have too little information to settle the question, and we have no reason to answer it anyway. All we need to know is that Shakespeare wrote both comedies and tragedies, as well as history plays, and in many cases his plays are hard to classify. Shakespeare was always ready to mix genres, sometimes blending history, comedy, *and* tragedy in the same play.

In his *Poetics*, the most important work of literary criticism ever written, Aristotle had described a tragedy as a play that moves an audience to feel "pity and fear" for the sufferings of its chief characters, who should be noble but imperfect figures whose flaws bring disaster on themselves. This little book had an enormous influence on Renaissance Europe, but whether it directly influenced Shakespeare is another unanswerable question. In any case Aristotle's preference for strict unity of plot and tone certainly failed to prevent the English playwright from combining tragedy with other elements. Followers of Aristotle often attacked Shakespeare for violating the Greek's prescriptions; many French critics even considered him vulgar!

The truth is that Shakespeare cares nothing for "unity" in the negative and narrow sense. He loves variety: the rich cast of characters, the opulent vocabulary, the complex plot, sudden alternations of tears and laughter, wild rhetoric, constant surprise. He seems to mock every notion of "rules" of drama. No playwright remotely like him, ancient or modern, had ever existed before. None has existed since. It seems safe to predict that none ever will.

No two of his plays are alike. He almost never repeated himself. Although his tragedies can be rich in humor, his comedies likewise contain much pathos, loss, and death. G. K. Chesterton, in the finest appreciation of *A Midsummer Night's Dream* ever written, summed up its spirit in one inspired phrase: "the mysticism of happiness." He added: "In pure poetry and the intoxication of words, Shakespeare never rose higher than he rises in this play." The whole play captures the atmosphere of an "exasperating dream," where nothing quite makes sense and every explanation only deepens the mystery. The plot is a labyrinth.

In contrast to Shakespeare's tragedies, the atmosphere of *A Midsummer Night's Dream* is more important than the characters, whom, except for Bottom, we hardly remember at all. None of them is serious in the way that Hamlet, Romeo, or even the heroes and heroines of the other great comedies are serious. It is no use analyzing them as if they were three-dimensional figures. We can hardly imagine them existing outside this play, or populating other plays. They belong here and nowhere else. They live only because the play lives. Like the dream it is, *A Midsummer Night's Dream* could never have a sequel!

ORDER AND CHAOS

Though Shakespeare's personal attitudes are often hard to identify, we can safely say that he loves order, harmony, music, and festivity. In that respect he is deeply conservative. He rejoices in the normal, the happy, in love, marriage, and childbirth. His plays are full of songs and dances, which are easy to overlook when we read them on the page. In none of his plays are music, songs, rhyme, dancing, and theater so dominant as in *A Midsummer Night's Dream*, where love really does conquer all under Puck's benign magic spells. Even Bottom rejoices in the arts, taking hilarious pride in his supposed gifts for acting and music.

His villains and troublemakers dislike these things. Egeus, in *A Midsummer Night's Dream*, demands his own daughter's death when she refuses to marry Demetrius, the man he has chosen for her. When the lovers triumph in spite of him, he vanishes from the play and is absent from the great wedding revels in the final act. It is hard to imagine Egeus enjoying Bottom's performance as Pyramus!

Generalizations about Shakespeare are usually risky, but he has no fondness for malcontents, either those who rigidly defend an old order or those who would damage or overturn it. Egeus is somewhat unusual in that he carries attachment to an old law to such an extreme that he becomes the play's malcontent.

> THE LUNATIC, THE LOVER, AND THE POET ARE OF IMAGINATION ALL COMPACT.

In Shakespeare there is always a sense that the world used to be better, that preventing its getting worse is the best we can hope for, and that there is no such thing as progress in the modern sense. Because of the world's natural tendency to worsen, to dissolve into chaos, with rightful kings often displaced by usurping tyrants, we must learn to be content with what we have. In Oberon and, especially, Puck, Shakespeare presents supernatural powers not as dark and ominous, but as positive, kindly, and humorous forces. The world is full of bad omens threatening chaos—storms, eclipses, wars, ghosts, witches, and prophecies—but we can preserve our most joyful experiences in festivities, celebration, music, drama, and the arts.

Nevertheless, Shakespeare's world is basically a happy one. If it seldom makes progress in our sense, if it is forever threatened by the abnormal, it also has a natural tendency to recover from tragedy and return to normal. Beauty may be temporarily destroyed by raw power, but it is always reborn. *A Midsummer Night's Dream* expresses the poet's sheer love of the normal more ecstatically than anything else he ever wrote. No wonder it has remained one of his most popular plays, inspiring other works of genius such as Felix Mendelssohn's glorious incidental music.

A CATHOLIC ANGLE?

Until now most scholars have assumed that Shakespeare had little to say about the events of his own time; in their view, he stayed carefully aloof from the raging political and religious disputes of his day and kept his opinions, if he had any, to himself. He was "universal," but only in a negative way, commenting on human nature but seldom if ever taking sides in the notable contemporary controversies that were splitting Elizabethan England and spilling much blood.

In 2005 Clare Asquith boldly challenged this view, expressed in all previous Shakespeare studies, in her amazing book *Shadowplay:*

"I KNOW A BANK WHERE THE WILD THYME BLOWS"

The Hidden Beliefs and Coded Politics of William Shakespeare. If her controversial thesis is widely accepted, we will have to adopt a truly revolutionary new approach to the Bard. Asquith is far from the first to detect Catholic sympathies in the great dramatist; G. K. Chesterton and many others have done so before her. But she has taken this immeasurably further than anyone else.

In her view Shakespeare was definitely a passionate Catholic, but, fearing persecution by the Tudor regime, which exerted tight censorship over the press and theater (the only media of his time), was forced to express his views in an extremely subtle code—so subtle, in fact, that virtually all readers and critics have missed it until now. Only in *Hamlet* does Shakespeare seem to show some awareness of the great issues of the Reformation, and even there he seems not to take sides. Asquith argues powerfully that, read carefully in its historical context, the play takes the Catholic side. She says the same is true of nearly all Shakespeare's plays, even those set in ancient Rome, pagan Britain, or on desert islands. To understand them we must "crack the code" that Shakespeare was forced to use in order to escape censorship.

How does this idea apply to *A Midsummer Night's Dream*? Here, if anywhere, is a play that seems to have nothing to do with the issues that divided Catholics and Protestants in the sixteenth century—a light comedy of lovers, fairies, and silly yokels set in a forest outside pre-Christian Athens. Nobody in the play says anything that is likely to remind us of the religious broils of Shakespeare's England many centuries later and thousands of miles away.

Of course this play, and all the others, may still be read in the traditional way, without any reference to the great wars of faith that divided the Christian world. But Asquith insists that if we read them that way, we are losing an essential dimension of their full meaning, because Shakespeare was a committed secret and illegal Catholic. He had to avoid persecution by writing his plays in a code that seemed to have nothing to do with religion, but which alert and sensitive Catholics in the audience might understand.

What was this code? According to Asquith the moon symbolized Queen Elizabeth and the new religion brought by her father, Henry VIII. For example, the opening lines of *A Midsummer Night's Dream*, spoken by Theseus, complain "how slow this old moon wanes." This statement would tip off Catholic spectators that the real subject was the old queen of England, whom, Catholics felt, had ruled the country for far too long.

Catholicism was symbolized by anything tall and fair, and Protestantism by the short and dark. The tall, fair Helena is symbolically Catholic, while Hermia, short and dark, is Protestant. The confusions of the four lovers become an allegory of England's religious strife, which Shakespeare hopes will end in reconciliation, just as the play ends in harmony.

Shakespeare himself, Asquith argues, appears as Bottom, hoping to please his rulers by entertaining them with a play. His very real fear of persecution is expressed comically in Bottom's seemingly absurd fear that he and his fellow actors may be "hanged" if they frighten the ladies in the audience.

In other plays, Asquith contends, an old order represents the Catholic England destroyed by Henry VIII and, currently, by his daughter Elizabeth. Even the plays set in ancient Rome before Julius Caesar overthrew the old

HENRY VIII.

THE PLAY *HENRY VIII* (ORIGINALLY CALLED *ALL IS TRUE*) WAS WRITTEN IN 1613 AND CAST THE TUDORS IN A NEAR-DIVINE LIGHT. DURING ITS PERFORMANCE IN JUNE OF THAT YEAR THE GLOBE BURNED TO THE GROUND.

HOW SLOW THIS OLD MOON WANES.

republic and replaced it with an empire were meant to stand for the older, Catholic England. Likewise all usurpers, such as Macbeth, or Claudius in *Hamlet*, are meant to remind Shakespeare's Catholic audience of the Tudor tyranny that was sill trying to stamp out the popular old religion of Catholicism in England.

According to Asquith, Shakespeare was playing a very dangerous game. Under the seemingly nonreligious surface of his plays, he was taking the side of that older religion and its traditions against the new regime of the Tudor dynasty. Most scholars have seen Shakespeare's attitude as vaguely conservative, but until now nobody has thought of him as such a passionate partisan of the old, pre-Tudor social and religious order. If she is right Asquith has given us a completely new conception of Shakespeare and a new key to interpreting his work, which nobody else has even suspected until now.

Chronology

1564   William Shakespeare is born on April 23 in Stratford-upon-Avon, England

1578-1582   Span of Shakespeare's "Lost Years," covering the time between leaving school and marrying Anne Hathaway of Stratford

1582   At age eighteen Shakespeare marries Anne Hathaway, age twenty-six, on November 28

1583   Susanna Shakespeare, William and Anne's first child, is born in May, six months after the wedding

1584   Birth of twins Hamnet and Judith Shakespeare

1585-1592   Shakespeare leaves his family in Stratford to become an actor and playwright in a London theater company

1587   Public beheading of Mary Queen of Scots

1593-94   The Bubonic (Black) Plague closes theaters in London

1594-96   As a leading playwright, Shakespeare creates some of his most popular work, including *A Midsummer Night's Dream* and *Romeo and Juliet*

1596   Hamnet Shakespeare dies in August at age eleven, possibly of plague

1596–97	*The Merchant of Venice* and *Henry IV, Part One* most likely are written
1599	The Globe Theater opens
1600	*Julius Caesar* is first performed at the Globe
1600–01	*Hamlet* is believed to have been written
1601–02	*Twelfth Night* is probably composed
1603	Queen Elizabeth dies; Scottish king James VI succeeds her and becomes England's James I
1604	Shakespeare pens *Othello*
1605	*Macbeth* is composed
1608–1610	London's theaters are forced to close when the plague returns and kills an estimated 33,000 people
1611	*The Tempest* is written
1613	The Globe Theater is destroyed by fire
1614	Reopening of the Globe
1616	Shakespeare dies on April 23
1623	Anne Hathaway, Shakespeare's widow, dies; a collection of Shakespeare's plays, known as the First Folio, is published

Source Notes

p. 10, par. 5, Asquith, Clare. *Shadowplay: The Hidden Beliefs and Coded Politics of William Shakespeare.* (New York: Public Affairs/Perseus Books Group, 2006).

p. 31, par. 2, Ben Jonson, "To the Memory of My Beloved, The Author, Mr. William Shakespeare, And What He Hath Left Us." In *Poetry X*, 4 Sep 2004, http://poetry.poetryx.com/poems/5271/

p. 39, par. 2, Spenser, Edmund. *The Faerie Queene.* (New York: Penguin Classics, 1979).

p. 88, par. 4, Aristotle, translated by S. H. Butcher. *Poetics.* (New York: Penguin Classics, 1997.); "pity and fear" is mentioned in section 1, part 4.

p. 89, par. 1, "The Mythical Sorrows of Shakespeare" by C.J. Sisson was delivered as the annual Shakespeare lecture of the British Academy in 1934.

p. 89, par. 3, G. K. Chesteron's essay on *A Midsummer Night's Dream* can be read at the American Chesterton Society's Web site, http://www.chesterton.org, by clicking on The Critic: A Midsummer Night's Dream.

P. 91, par. 4, Asquith, Ibid.

A Shakespeare Glossary

The student should not try to memorize these, but only refer to them as needed. We can never stress enough that the best way to learn Shakespeare's language is simply to *hear* it—to hear it spoken well by good actors. After all, small children master every language on earth through their ears, without studying dictionaries, and we should master Shakespeare, as much as possible, the same way.

addition —a name or title (knight, duke, duchess, king, etc.)

admire —to marvel

affect —to like or love; to be attracted to

an —if ("An I tell you that, I'll be hanged.")

approve —to prove or confirm

attend —to pay attention

belike —probably

beseech —to beg or request

betimes —soon; early

bondman —a slave

bootless —futile; useless; in vain

broil —a battle

charge —expense, responsibility; to command or accuse

clepe, clept —to name; named

common —of the common people; below the nobility

conceit —imagination

condition —social rank; quality

countenance —face; appearance; favor

cousin —a relative

cry you mercy —beg your pardon

curious —careful; attentive to detail

dear —expensive

discourse —to converse; conversation

discover —to reveal or uncover

dispatch —to speed or hurry; to send; to kill

doubt —to suspect

entreat —to beg or appeal

envy —to hate or resent; hatred; resentment

ere —before

ever, e'er —always

eyne —eyes

fain —gladly

fare —to eat; to prosper

favor —face, privilege

fellow —a peer or equal

filial —of a child toward its parent

fine —an end; in fine = in sum

fond —foolish

fool —a darling

genius —a good or evil spirit

gentle —well-bred; not common;

gentleman —one whose labor was done by servants (Note: to call someone a *gentleman* was not a mere compliment on his manners; it meant that he was above the common people.)

gentles —people of quality

get —to beget (a child)

go to —"go on"; "come off it"

go we —let us go

haply —perhaps

happily —by chance; fortunately

hard by —nearby

heavy —sad or serious

husbandry —thrift; economy

instant —immediate

kind —one's nature; species

knave —a villain; a poor man

lady —a woman of high social rank (Note: *lady* was not a synonym for *woman* or *polite woman*; it was not a compliment, but, like *gentleman*, simply a word referring to one's actual legal status in society.)

leave — permission; "take my leave" = depart (with permission)

lief, lieve —"I had as lief" = I would just as soon; I would rather

like —to please; "it likes me not" = it is disagreeable to me

livery —the uniform of a nobleman's servants; emblem

mark —notice; pay attention

morrow —morning

needs —necessarily

nice —too fussy or fastidious

owe —to own

passing —very

peculiar —individual; exclusive

privy —private; secret

proper —handsome; one's very own ("his proper son")

protest —to insist or declare

quite —completely

require —request

several —different, various;

severally —separately

sirrah —a term used to address social inferiors

sooth —truth

state —condition; social rank

still —always; persistently

success —result(s)

surfeit —fullness

touching —concerning; about; as for

translate —to transform

unfold —to disclose

villain —a low or evil person; originally, a peasant

voice —a vote; consent; approval

vouchsafe —to confide or grant

vulgar —common

want —to lack

weeds —clothing

what ho —"hello, there!"

wherefore —why

wit —intelligence; sanity

withal —moreover; nevertheless

without —outside

would —wish

Suggested Essay Topics

1. Do you think any of the characters of *A Midsummer Night's Dream* speak for Shakespeare? Why or why not?

2. What does Theseus tell us, and illustrate, about the nature of a wise ruler?

3. How does Bottom, a mere weaver, "steal" the play from the other, seemingly more important characters?

4. Pagan gods such as Venus, Cupid, Phoebe, and Neptune are often mentioned but never actually appear in the play. How do they influence the events of the story?

Testing Your Memory

1. Puck replaces Bottom's head with that of
   a) a dog; b) a lion; c) an ass; d) a bear.

2. Bottom and his friends act out the story of
   a) Romeo and Juliet; b) Pyramus and Thisby; c) Antony and
   Cleopatra; d) Adam and Eve.

3. Theseus is a) king of the forest; b) duke of Athens;
   c) emperor of Rome; d) a Greek god.

4. Hippolyta is a) queen of the Amazons;
   b) princess of Egypt; c) duchess of York d) a rich widow.

5. Oberon is
   a) a carpenter; b) king of the fairies; c) an elf; d) a hunter.

6. After his transformation, Bottom feels a sudden craving for
   a) hay; b) wine; c) beef; d) salt water.

7. When Lysander is under Puck's spell, he
   a) thinks he is mad; b) runs away from Athens; c) decides to find
   Bottom; d) falls in love with Helena.

8. Puck is also known as
   a) Robin Goodfellow; b) Cupid; c) a mermaid; d) Peter Quince.

9. Egeus asks Theseus to
   a) delay his wedding to Hippolyta; b) force Hermia to marry
   Demetrius; c) kill Lysander; d) cancel the play.

10. Bottom likes music, especially
    a) the harp; b) violins; c) tongs and bones; d) the fairy chorus.

11. When the play is performed, one of the actors plays
    a) Hamlet; b) the king; c) a fairy; d) moonshine.

12. Oberon and Titania quarrel over
    a) a little boy; b) Bottom; c) Puck; d) Thisby.

13. Bottom calls the play he stars in
    a) a tragedy; b) a comedy; c) a satire; d) a musical.

14. The actors are afraid of
    a) making Theseus angry; b) not being funny; c) frightening the ladies; d) the lion.

15. Back to normal, Bottom thinks he has
    a) seen ghosts; b) met Puck; c) become a great actor; d) had a beautiful dream.

16. After learning of the planned elopement, Helena decides to
    a) tell Demetrius; b) steal Lysander from Hermia; c) seek the fairies; d) play a prank on Bottom's friends.

17. According to Helena, Cupid is said to be
    a) cruel; b) musical; c) untrustworthy; d) blind.

18. Titania thinks Bottom is
    a) in disguise; b) wise and beautiful; c) ignorant; d) a fairy.

19. Oberon tells Puck that he has actually seen
    a) Cupid; b) Theseus; c) Bottom; d) a sea monster.

20. Hippolyta thinks Bottom's play is
    a) deeply moving; b) silly; c) too long; d) obscene.

Answer Key

1. c; 2. b; 3. b; 4. a; 5. b; 6. a; 7. d; 8. a; 9. b; 10. c; 11. d;
12. a; 13. b; 14. c; 15. d; 16. a; 17. d; 18. b; 19. a; 20. b

Further Information

BOOKS

Ackroyd, Peter. *Shakespeare: The Biography*. New York: Nan A. Talese, 2005.

Dunton-Downer, Leslie, and Alan Riding. *The Essential Shakespeare Handbook*. New York: Dorling-Kindersley, 2004.

Manga Shakespeare series. *A Midsummer Night's Dream*. New York: Harry N. Abrams/Amulet, 2008.

New Folger Library Shakespeare. *A Midsummer Night's Dream*. New York: Washington Square Press, 2004.

WEB SITES

Absolute Shakespeare is a resource for the Bard's plays, sonnets, and poems and includes summaries, quotes, films, trivia, and more. http://absoluteshakespeare.com

Play Shakespeare: The Ultimate Free Shakespeare Resource features all the play texts with an online glossary, reviews, a discussion forum, and links to festivals worldwide. http://www.playshakespeare.com

William Shakespeare Info: *A Midsummer Night's Dream* provides a vast collection of links related to the specific play, as well as articles about Shakespeare's life, world, and works. http://www.william-shakespeare.info/shakespeare-play-a-midsummer-nights-dream.htm

FILMS

A Midsummer Night's Dream, directed by Max Reinhardt; with James Cagney, Olivia DeHaviland, and Mickey Rooney, 1935.

A Midsummer Night's Dream, directed by Peter Hall; with David Warner, Diana Rigg, Judi Dench, and Helen Mirren, 1968.

A Midsummer Night's Dream, directed by Michael Hoffman; with Kevin Kline, Michelle Pfeiffer, and Stanley Tucci, 1999.

AUDIO BOOK

A Midsummer Night's Dream, Naxos AudioBooks; with Warren Mitchell as Bottom, Michael Maloney as Oberon, and Sarah Woodward as Titania.

RECORDING

A Midsummer Night's Dream, Caedmon; with Paul Scofield, Joy Parker, and Stanley Holloway.

Bibliography

General Commentary

Bate, Jonathan, and Eric Rasmussen, eds. *William Shakespeare Complete Works (Modern Library)*. New York: Random House, 2007.

Bloom, Harold. *Shakespeare: The Invention of the Human*. New York: Riverhead Books,1998.

Garber, Marjorie. *Shakespeare After All*. New York: Pantheon, 2004.

Goddard, Harold C. *The Meaning of Shakespeare*. Chicago: University of Chicago Press, 1951.

Traversi, D. L. *An Approach to Shakespeare*. Palo Alto, CA: Stanford University Press, 1957.

Van Doren, Mark. *Shakespeare*. Garden City, NY: Doubleday, 1939.

Biography

Burgess, Anthony. *Shakespeare*. New York: Alfred A. Knopf, 1970.

Chute, Marchette. *Shakespeare of London*. New York: Dutton, 1949.

Greenblatt, Stephen. *Will in the World: How Shakespeare Became Shakespeare*. New York: W. W. Norton & Company, 2004.

Honan, Park. *Shakespeare: A Life*. New York: Oxford University Press, 1998.

Schoenbaum, Samuel. *William Shakespeare: A Documentary Life*. New York: Oxford University Press, 1975.

———. *William Shakespeare: Records and Images*. New York: Oxford University Press, 1981.

Index

Page numbers in **boldface** are illustrations.

About the Author

Joseph Sobran is the author of several books, including *Alias Shakespeare* (1997). He lives in northern Virginia.